MARCIA G[...]

LOUIS B. WRIGHT, General Editor. Director of the Folger Shakespeare Library from 1948 until his retirement in 1968, Dr. Wright has devoted over forty years to the study of the Shakespearean period. In 1926 he completed his doctoral thesis on "Vaudeville Elements in Elizabethan Drama" and subsequently published many articles on the stagecraft and theatre of Shakespeare's day. He is the author of *Middle-Class Culture in Elizabethan England* (1935), *Religion and Empire* (1942), *The Elizabethans' America* (1965), and many other books and essays on the history and literature of the Tudor and Stuart periods, including *Shakespeare for Everyman* (1964). Dr. Wright has taught at the universities of North Carolina, California at Los Angeles, Michigan, Minnesota, and other American institutions. From 1932 to 1948 he was instrumental in developing the research program of the Henry E. Huntington Library and Art Gallery. During his tenure as Director, the Folger Shakespeare Library became one of the leading research institutions of the world for the study of the backgrounds of Anglo-American civilization.

VIRGINIA A. LaMAR, Assistant Editor. A member of the staff of the Folger Shakespeare Library from 1946 until her death in 1968, Miss LaMar served as research assistant to the Director and as Executive Secretary. Prior to 1946 Miss LaMar had been a secretary in the British Admiralty Delegation in Washington, D.C., receiving the King's Medal in 1945 for her services. She was coeditor of the *Historie of Travell into Virginia Britania* by William Strachey, published by The Hakluyt Society in 1953, and author of *English Dress in the Age of Shakespeare* and *Travel and Roads in England* in the "Folger Booklets on Tudor and Stuart Civilization" series.

The Folger Shakespeare Library

GENERAL EDITOR

LOUIS B. WRIGHT

Director, Folger Shakespeare Library, 1948–1968

•

ASSISTANT EDITOR

VIRGINIA A. LaMAR

Executive Secretary, Folger Shakespeare Library, 1946–1968

THE TRAGEDY OF

JULIUS CAESAR

By

WILLIAM

SHAKESPEARE

WASHINGTON SQUARE PRESS

THE TRAGEDY OF JULIUS CÆSAR

A *Washington Square Press* edition
1st printing.....................November, 1958
22nd printing........................June, 1969

A new edition of a distinguished literary work now made available in an inexpensive, well-designed format

L

Published by Washington Square Press,
a division of Simon & Schuster, Inc., 630 Fifth Avenue, New York, N.Y.

Washington Square Press editions are distributed in the U.S. by Simon & Schuster, Inc., 630 Fifth Avenue, New York, N.Y. 10020 and in Canada by Simon & Schuster of Canada, Ltd., Richmond Hill, Ontario, Canada.

Standard Book Number: 671-45715-2.

Preface

This edition of *The Tragedy of Julius Cæsar* is designed to make available a readable text of one of Shakespeare's most popular plays. In the centuries since Shakespeare many changes have occurred in the meanings of words, and some clarification of Shakespeare's vocabulary may be helpful. To provide the reader with necessary notes in the most accessible format, we have placed them on the pages facing the text that they explain. We have tried to make these notes as brief and simple as possible. Preliminary to the text we have also included a brief statement of essential information about Shakespeare and his stage. Readers desiring more detailed information should refer to the books suggested in the references, and if still further information is needed, the bibliographies in those books will provide the necessary clues to the literature of the subject.

The early texts of all of Shakespeare's plays provide only inadequate stage directions, and it is conventional for modern editors to add many that clarify the action. Such additions, and additions to entrances, are placed in square brackets.

All illustrations are from material in the Folger Library collections.

L. B. W.
V. A. L.

May 14, 1958

The Appeal of Roman History

When Shakespeare picked up his Plutarch and began to dig out material for a play about Julius Cæsar, he had just finished *Henry V* and the problems of presenting history on the stage were still uppermost in his mind. Though Shakespeare's *Julius Cæsar* is classified as a tragedy, it retains structural affinities with the history plays and lacks the concentration upon a single tragic hero demanded of classical tragedy. There is good evidence to believe that Shakespeare wrote *Henry V* early in 1599 and that it was performed at the Globe in the summer of the same year. The rapidity with which the popular chronicle play about an English hero-king was followed by *Julius Cæsar*, which a German traveler, Dr. Thomas Platter, saw performed on September 21, 1599, will help to explain why the new play has the episodic structure characteristic of Elizabethan historical drama. Though the acting company probably felt that it needed a tragedy, and Shakespeare was doing his best to supply one, he could not quite free himself from the techniques of the loose-hung history play that had already proved a stage success. And though *Julius Cæsar* is also so loosely put together that critics still debate as to whether Shakespeare meant to make Brutus or Cæsar the hero of the piece, it too was popular from the beginning and has consistently held the stage ever since.

The ordinary spectator in the theatre is not much concerned about the fine points of structural analysis so beloved by critics. The Elizabethan playgoer cared little whether Shakespeare remembered the rules for classical tragedy, provided that he wrote a vivid drama about some episode that interested him, and the life of Cæsar was clearly of interest, almost as pertinent as that of an English king.

Roman history was widely read in Shakespeare's age. Every boy who went through the grammar school gained an acquaintance with the history of Rome along with other training in Latin literature. The Elizabethans believed that history, particularly classical history, was useful for the lessons that a reader might glean from it. Political wisdom especially was to be found in the Roman historians. Since only those learned enough to read Latin could unlock these stores of wisdom in the original language, translators early began to make Roman history available in English versions. In 1579, Sir Thomas North published his translation (made from Jacques Amyot's French text) of Plutarch's *Lives of the Noble Grecians and Romans,* which had at least eight editions and issues by 1631. This was a large folio volume, heavy and ponderous to handle, but eminently readable, and Shakespeare and his contemporaries got much of their classical information from it. Plutarch was Shakespeare's main source for *Julius Cæsar.*

In addition to North's translation of Plutarch, Shakespeare's contemporaries had available translations of Livy, Tacitus, Polybius, Appian, Cæsar, Suetonius, and others. Compilations of the facts of Roman history were prepared for ready reference and handbooks of history contained many scraps of information about the Romans. Lodowick Lloyd published a miscellany of classical history which he called *The Consent of Time* (1590) and William Fulbecke brought out a condensation of Roman history entitled *An Historical Collection of the Continual Factions, Tumults and Massacres of the Romans and Italians . . . before the Peaceable Empire of Augustus Cæsar* (1601). Richard Reynolds brought out as early as 1571 *A Chronicle of All the Noble Emperors of the Romans from Julius Cæsar*, with the avowed purpose of providing a mirror in which princes and others might see the virtues and vices of the ancients. The Elizabethans did not lack for information about Roman history, and countless allusions testify to their knowledge.

The modern world may have forgotten the enormous respect that the sixteenth and seventeenth centuries had for classical civilization. The great outburst of intellectual activity that stirred all of Europe in the period that we call the Renaissance had its inception in the belief that classical learning and classical literature would have a humanizing and civilizing influence of vast benefit to mankind. The Greek and Roman classics became the basis of education and everyone who hoped to achieve any reputation for cultivation was expected to know them. Even those who could make no pretense to learning picked up scraps of classical lore, for inevitably stories and incidents from the ancient past became part of a well-worn tradition. The least enlightened grocer's apprentice of London had probably seen Julius Cæsar among the Nine Worthies in some pageant or procession and had recognized him for a great Roman hero.

The choice of Julius Cæsar as a subject for a play

to follow *Henry V* is not hard to understand. On the Continent, in the English universities, and on the English public stages, plays dealing with Julius Cæsar had been acted long before Shakespeare's play appeared. There is no evidence, however, that Shakespeare used any of these earlier plays in writing his own work. In Plutarch's lives of Cæsar, Brutus, and Antony he found abundant material and in a few instances he took passages from North's translation almost word for word.

As for the history, he condensed and telescoped it to suit his purposes. Cæsar's triumph, which Shakespeare places at the opening of the play on the Feast of Lupercalia, February 15 in the year 44 B.C., actually occurred in October of the previous year. In the play, the Battle of Philippi seems to take place very shortly after Cæsar's murder at some nearby place. Actually there were two battles more than two weeks apart, fought in Macedonia, late in the year 42 B.C. Shakespeare the dramatist was not careful about historical details any more than he was concerned about historical anachronisms. If he needed a clock to strike the hour in Rome, he let a clock strike, and nobody bothered to inquire about when striking clocks were invented.

Although some critics have argued that Shakespeare's play has two heroes, Brutus and Cæsar, Shakespeare undoubtedly meant to focus interest on the traditional hero, Cæsar. As George Lyman Kittredge and others have pointed out, Cæsar does not vanish from the play with his murder in the first scene of Act III, but his spirit hovers over the rest of the play, and his ghost, like the conventional ghost in the popular revenge plays of the day, returns to wreak vengeance on his antagonists.

To the Elizabethans, Cæsar was a character of consuming interest. They were vastly interested in strong men who could impose order in a chaotic world. We should remember that civil war and social chaos had been the state of England in the years before the rise of the Tudors, and Englishmen particularly valued the stability that Queen Elizabeth and her predecessors had established, as they feared a return of strife if she died without a settled succession. Cæsar had been a leader with the capacity for rule such as the Elizabethans understood and approved. They did not have our modern distaste for dictators, for the days of Mussolini and Hitler were still some centuries ahead, and they admired forceful and successful leaders like Cæsar, as they admired Henry V, Henry VII, Henry VIII, and their own Queen. If Cæsar on Shakespeare's stage sounds pompous to us, his manner was not objectionable to the spectator at the Globe. It was the manner that an Elizabethan would expect of one who had conquered most of the known world.

When the United States was a very new nation, the fathers of the country looked back upon republican Rome for examples of virtue and patriotism. George Washington was often called Cincinnatus after one of the primitive Roman heroes, and the officers of the Revolution who organized into a veterans' group could think of no name that better connoted their patriotic ideals than the Society of the Cincinnati. On the contrary, the Elizabethans looked back to imperial Rome for inspiration. Although they gave lip service, it is true, to the ideals of the Roman republic, their primary interest was in the great days of the Roman Empire. Although Julius Cæsar technically lived and died in the later years of the Roman republic, the Elizabethans looked upon him as the progenitor of the great line of Cæsars, the emperors who brought glory to Rome and the Pax Romana to all the world. Shakespeare demonstrated the shrewd judgment of a successful playwright in choosing Julius Cæsar as the subject of a play.

THE ENDURING INTEREST IN THE PLAY

But since Shakespeare always transcends the mere appraisal of a probable success at the box office, he wrote in *Julius Cæsar* a play that possessed elements of enduring interest. The dramatist found himself concerned with a study in character and he brought the major figures in the play to life with such vividness that the qualities that he attributed to them have become invincibly fixed in the consciousness of later ages. As Shakespeare created for the future an interpretation of the history of the Wars of the Roses, so he shaped the future interpretation of the last days of the Roman republic and the characters who played their roles in it. If the average American of our time thinks of Cæsar, Brutus, Cassius, or Mark Antony, he visualizes him in Shakespeare's characterization.

Brutus is the noble patriot, filled with memories of a great patriot-ancestor whom he must emulate. If to us he seems stuffy and self-consciously virtuous, the audience who first listened to his lines probably approved of his sententious utterances, so like axioms they had often heard. He represents the contemplative type and, ironically, his decisions, reached with so much show of justice and wisdom, usually turn out to be the wrong ones. Cassius, on the other hand, is more Machiavellian; he is the "lean and hungry" type of introspective thinker who instinctively knows what ruthless measures are necessary but allows himself to be talked out of them by Brutus' show of virtuous wisdom. Mark Antony in this play is presented as the master politician, possessed of both shrewdness and eloquence. That he is a lover of pleasure, gaiety, and luxury is made clear, but it remains for a later play to show him as a victim of these weaknesses. At the moment he is a supple politician and a good soldier able to hold his own with Octavius, who is to become the great Augustus Cæsar.

The interplay of these personalities clearly fascinated Shakespeare as it has fascinated actors and readers of *Julius Cæsar* ever since. In this play an actor's ambition is satisfied with something besides the title role; other parts are as good or better. Any actor can rejoice at success in the roles of Brutus, Cassius, or Antony. Only the female roles are slight, for this is a play with little feminine interest, and we cannot get excited about either Portia or Calpurnia, the only women in the cast.

That *Julius Cæsar* made a great impression upon contemporary audiences is clear from allusions in the literature of the period. Apparently it had frequent revivals and it was acted at Court before James I and later before Charles I. After the Restoration of Charles II it was one of the plays of Shakespeare that returned to the stage in its original form instead of in an adaptation. Thomas Betterton, the veteran Shakespearean acror, won Colley Cibber's praise for the dignity and convincing quality of his acting in the part of Brutus in the 1680's. The play remained a popular stage piece for many years, and Betterton himself, who lived on until 1710, continued to act Brutus until near the end of his career.

Throughout most of the eighteenth century, *Julius Cæsar* was periodically revived, and most of the great actors of that century with the exception of Garrick distinguished themselves in one or another of the roles. In the American colonies, traveling dramatic companies had *Julius Cæsar* in their repertories, and toward the end of the eighteenth century it was much read and quoted. The first six Shakespearean quotations in Thomas Jefferson's commonplace book were from *Julius Cæsar*. Abigail Adams, who liked to quote Shakespeare in letters to John Adams, her husband, drew selections from *Julius Cæsar* and sometimes used the name of Brutus' heroic wife Portia as a signature.

Through most of the nineteenth and twentieth centuries, on both sides of the Atlantic, *Julius Cæsar* enjoyed frequent performances. It was said that few actors rose to distinction as tragedians without at some time playing the role of Cassius, Brutus, or Antony. In the secondary schools for many years *Julius Cæsar* was a favorite play for study and for acting. During the nineteenth century, when reciting set speeches was a part of educational training, not many schoolboys escaped the ordeal of learning and delivering Mark Antony's oration over the dead Cæsar. Few plays have been so widely read and played over so long a period. Everyone in every age since its composition

has been able to find something of interest in this
remarkable drama.

THE TEXT

The first printing of *Julius Cæsar* occurred in the
First Folio of 1623. The Second, Third, and Fourth
Folios reprinted the text of the First Folio without any
substantial changes and the play presents few textual
problems. Approximately a dozen corrections, suggested
by later editors and now generally accepted, have been
adopted in the present text.

THE AUTHOR

Even before the first recorded performance of *Julius
Cæsar*, Shakespeare was so well known as a literary and
dramatic craftsman that Francis Meres, a young preach-
er, in a volume called *Palladis Tamia: Wits Treasury*
(1598), referred in flattering terms to him as "mel-
lifluous and honey-tongued Shakespeare," famous for his
Venus and Adonis, his *Lucrece,* and "his sugared sonnets," which were circulating "among his private
friends." Meres observes further that "as Plautus and
Seneca are accounted the best for comedy and tragedy
among the Latins, so Shakespeare among the English
is the most excellent in both kinds for the stage," and he
mentions a dozen plays that had made a name for
Shakespeare. He concludes with the remark "that the
Muses would speak with Shakespeare's fine filed phrase
if they would speak English."

To those acquainted with the history of the Elizabethan and Jacobean periods, it is incredible that anyone should be so naïve or ignorant as to doubt the reality

of Shakespeare as the author of the plays that bear his name. Yet so much nonsense has been written about other "candidates" for the plays that it is well to remind readers that no credible evidence that would stand up in a court of law has ever been adduced to prove either that Shakespeare did not write his plays or that anyone else wrote them. All the theories offered for the authorship of Francis Bacon, the Earl of Derby, the Earl of Oxford, the Earl of Hertford, Christopher Marlowe, and a score of other candidates are mere conjectures spun from the active imaginations of persons who confuse hypothesis and conjecture with evidence.

As Meres' statement of 1598 indicates, Shakespeare was already a popular playwright whose name carried weight at the box office. The obvious reputation of Shakespeare as early as 1598 makes the effort to prove him a myth one of the most absurd in the history of human perversity.

The anti-Shakespeareans talk darkly about a plot of vested interests to maintain the authorship of Shakespeare. Nobody has any vested interest in Shakespeare, but every scholar is interested in the truth and in the quality of evidence advanced by special pleaders who set forth hypotheses in place of facts.

The anti-Shakespeareans base their arguments upon a few simple premises, all of them false. These false premises are that Shakespeare was an unlettered yokel without any schooling, that nothing is known about Shakespeare, and that only a noble lord or the equivalent in background could have written the plays. The facts are that more is known about Shakespeare than about most dramatists of his day, that he had a very good education, acquired in the Stratford Grammar

School, that the plays show no evidence of profound book learning, and that the knowledge of kings and courts evident in the plays is no greater than any intelligent young man could have picked up at second hand. Most anti-Shakespeareans are naïve and betray an obvious snobbery. The author of their favorite plays, they imply, must have had a college diploma framed and hung on his study wall like the one in their dentist's office, and obviously so great a writer must have had a title or some equally significant evidence of exalted social background. They forget that genius has a way of cropping up in unexpected places and that none of the great creative writers of the world got his inspiration in a college or university course.

William Shakespeare was the son of John Shakespeare of Stratford-upon-Avon, a substantial citizen of that small but busy market town in the center of the rich agricultural county of Warwick. John Shakespeare kept a shop, what we would call a general store; he dealt in wool and other produce and gradually acquired property. As a youth, John Shakespeare had learned the trade of glover and leather worker. There is no contemporary evidence that the elder Shakespeare was a butcher, though the anti-Shakespeareans like to talk about the ignorant "butcher's boy of Stratford." Their only evidence is a statement by gossipy John Aubrey, more than a century after William Shakespeare's birth, that young William followed his father's trade and when he killed a calf "he would do it in a high style and make a speech." We would like to believe the story true, but Aubrey is not a very credible witness.

John Shakespeare probably continued to operate a farm at Snitterfield that his father had leased. He married Mary Arden, daughter of his father's landlord, a man of some property. The third of their eight children was William, baptized on April 26, 1564, and probably born three days before. At least it is conventional to celebrate April 23 as his birthday.

The Stratford records give considerable information about John Shakespeare. We know that he held several municipal offices including those of alderman and mayor. In 1580 he was in some sort of legal difficulty and was fined for neglecting a summons of the Court of Queen's Bench requiring him to appear at Westminster and be bound over to keep the peace.

As a citizen and alderman of Stratford, John Shakespeare was entitled to send his son to the grammar school free. Though the records are lost, there can be no reason to doubt that this is where young William received his education. As any student of the period knows, the grammar schools provided the basic education in Latin learning and literature. The Elizabethan grammar school is not to be confused with modern grammar schools. Many cultivated men of the day received all their formal education in the grammar schools. At the universities in this period a student would have received little training that would have inspired him to be a creative writer. At Stratford young Shakespeare would have acquired a familiarity with Latin and some little knowledge of Greek. He would have read Latin authors and become acquainted with the plays of Plautus and Terence. Undoubtedly in this period of his life he received that stimulation to read and explore for himself the world of ancient and modern history which he later utilized in his plays. The youngster who does not acquire this type of intellectual curiosity *before* college days rarely develops as a result of a college course the kind of mind Shakespeare demonstrated. His learning in books was anything but profound, but he clearly had the probing curiosity that sent him in search of information, and he had a keenness in the observation of nature and of humankind that finds reflection in his poetry.

There is little documentation for Shakespeare's boyhood. There is little reason why there should be. Nobody knew that he was going to be a dramatist about whom any scrap of information would be prized in the centuries to come. He was merely an active and vigorous youth of Stratford, perhaps assisting his father in his business, and no Boswell bothered to write down facts about him. The most important record that we have is a marriage license issued by the Bishop of Worcester on November 28, 1582, to permit William Shakespeare to marry Anne Hathaway, seven or eight years his senior; furthermore, the Bishop permitted the marriage after reading the banns only once instead of three times, evidence of the desire for haste. The need was explained on May 26, 1583, when the christening of Susanna, daughter of William and Anne Shakespeare, was recorded at Stratford. Two years later, on February 2, 1585, the records show the birth of twins to the Shakespeares, a boy and a girl who were christened Hamnet and Judith.

What William Shakespeare was doing in Stratford during the early years of his married life, or when he went to London, we do not know. It has been conjectured that he tried his hand at school teaching, but that is a mere guess. There is a legend that he left Stratford to escape a charge of poaching in the park of Sir Thomas

Lucy of Charlecote, but there is no proof of this. There is also a legend that when first he came to London he earned his living by holding horses outside a playhouse and presently was given employment inside, but there is nothing better than eighteenth-century hearsay for this. How Shakespeare broke into the London theatres as a dramatist and actor we do not know. But lack of information is not surprising, for Elizabethans did not write their autobiographies, and we know even less about the lives of many writers and some men of affairs than we know about Shakespeare. By 1592 he was so well established and popular that he incurred the envy of the dramatist and pamphleteer Robert Greene, who referred to him as an "upstart crow . . . in his own conceit the only Shake-scene in a country." From this time onward contemporary allusions and references in legal documents enable the scholar to chart Shakespeare's career with greater accuracy than is possible with most other Elizabethan dramatists.

By 1594 Shakespeare was a member of the company of actors known as the Lord Chamberlain's Men. After the accession of James I, in 1603, the company would have the sovereign for their patron and would be known as the King's Men. During the period of its greatest prosperity, this company would have as its principal theatres the Globe and the Blackfriars. Shakespeare was both an actor and a shareholder in the company. Tradition has assigned him such acting roles as Adam in *As You Like It* and the Ghost in *Hamlet,* a modest place on the stage that suggests that he may have had other duties in the management of the company. Such conclusions, however, are based on surmise.

What we do know is that his plays were popular and

that he was highly successful in his vocation. His first play may have been *The Comedy of Errors,* acted perhaps in 1591. Certainly this was one of his earliest plays. The three parts of *Henry VI* were acted sometime between 1590 and 1592. Critics are not in agreement about precisely how much Shakespeare wrote of these three plays. *Richard III* probably dates from 1593. With this play Shakespeare captured the imagination of Elizabethan audiences, then enormously interested in historical plays. With *Richard III*, Shakespeare also gave an interpretation pleasing to the Tudors of the rise to power of the grandfather of Queen Elizabeth. From this time onward, Shakespeare's plays followed on the stage in rapid succession: *Titus Andronicus, The Taming of the Shrew, The Two Gentlemen of Verona, Love's Labour's Lost, Romeo and Juliet, Richard II, A Midsummer Night's Dream, King John, The Merchant of Venice, Henry IV*, Pts. I and II, *Much Ado About Nothing, Henry V, Julius Cæsar, As You Like It, Twelfth Night, Hamlet, The Merry Wives of Windsor, All's Well That Ends Well, Measure for Measure, Othello, King Lear,* and nine others that followed before Shakespeare retired completely, about 1613.

In the course of his career in London, he made enough money to enable him to retire to Stratford with a competence. His purchase on May 4, 1597, of New Place, then the second largest dwelling in Stratford, a "pretty house of brick and timber," with a handsome garden, indicates his increasing prosperity. There his wife and children lived while he busied himself in the London theatres. The summer before he acquired New Place, his life was darkened by the death of his only son, Hamnet, a child of eleven. In May, 1602, Shakespeare purchased one hundred and seven acres of fertile farmland near Stratford and a few months later bought a cottage and garden across the alley from New Place. About 1611, he seems to have returned permanently to Stratford, for the next year a legal document refers to him as "William Shakespeare of Stratford-upon-Avon . . . gentleman." To achieve the desired appellation of gentleman, William Shakespeare had seen to it that the College of Heralds in 1596 granted his father a coat of arms. In one step he thus became a second-generation gentleman.

Shakespeare's daughter Susanna made a good match in 1607 with Dr. John Hall, a prominent and prosperous Stratford physician. His second daughter, Judith, did not marry until she was thirty-two years old, and then, under somewhat scandalous circumstances, she married Thomas Quiney, a Stratford vintner. On March 25, 1616, Shakespeare made his will, bequeathing his landed property to Susanna, £300 to Judith, certain sums to other relatives, and his second-best bed to his wife, Anne. Much has been made of the second-best bed, but the legacy probably indicates only that Anne liked that particular bed. Shakespeare, following the practice of the time, may have already arranged with Susanna for his wife's care. Finally, on April 23, 1616, the anniversary of his birth, William Shakespeare died, and he was buried on April 25 within the chancel of Trinity Church, as befitted an honored citizen. On August 6, 1623, a few months before the publication of the collected edition of Shakespeare's plays, Anne Shakespeare joined her husband in death.

During his lifetime Shakespeare made no effort to publish any of his plays, though eighteen appeared in print in single-play editions known as quartos. Some of these are corrupt versions known as "bad quartos." No quarto, so far as is known, had the author's approval. Plays were not considered "literature" any more than radio and television scripts today are considered literature. Dramatists sold their plays outright to the theatrical companies and it was usually considered in the company's interest to keep plays from getting into print. To achieve a reputation as a man of letters, Shakespeare wrote his *Sonnets* and his narrative poems, *Venus and Adonis* and *The Rape of Lucrece*, but he probably never dreamed that his plays would establish his reputation as a literary genius. Only Ben Jonson, a man known for his colossal conceit, had the crust to call his plays *Works*, as he did when he published an edition in 1616. But men laughed at Ben Jonson.

After Shakespeare's death, two of his old colleagues in the King's Men, John Heminges and Henry Condell, decided that it would be a good thing to print, in more accurate versions than were then available, the plays already published and eighteen additional plays not previously published in quarto. In 1623 appeared *Mr. William Shakespeares Comedies, Histories, & Tragedies. Published according to the True Originall Copies. London. Printed by Isaac Iaggard and Ed. Blount.* This was the famous First Folio, a work that had the authority of Shakespeare's associates. The only play commonly attributed to Shakespeare that was omitted in the First Folio was *Pericles*. In their preface, "To the great

Variety of Readers," Heminges and Condell state that whereas "you were abused with diverse stolen and surreptitious copies, maimed and deformed by the frauds and stealths of injurious impostors that exposed them, even those are now offered to your view cured and perfect of their limbs; and all the rest, absolute in their numbers, as he conceived them." What they used for printer's copy is one of the vexed problems of scholarship, and skilled bibliographers have devoted years of study to the question of the relation of the "copy" for the First Folio to Shakespeare's manuscripts. In some cases it is clear that the editors corrected printed quarto versions of the plays, probably by comparison with playhouse scripts. Whether these scripts were in Shakespeare's autograph is anybody's guess. No manuscript of any play in Shakespeare's handwriting has survived. Indeed, very few play manuscripts from this period by any author are extant. The Tudor and Stuart periods had not yet learned to prize autographs and authors' original manuscripts.

Since the First Folio contains eighteen plays not previously printed, it is the only source for these. For the other eighteen, which had appeared in quarto versions, the First Folio also had the authority of an edition prepared and overseen by Shakespeare's colleagues and professional associates. But since editorial standards in 1623 were far from strict, and Heminges and Condell were actors rather than editors by profession, the texts are sometimes careless. The printing and proofreading of the First Folio also left much to be desired, and some garbled passages have to be corrected and emended. The "good quarto" texts have to be taken into account in preparing a modern edition.

Because of the great popularity of Shakespeare through the centuries, the First Folio has become a prized book, but it is not a very rare one, for it is estimated that 238 copies are extant. The Folger Shakespeare Library in Washington, D.C., has seventy-nine copies of the First Folio, collected by the founder, Henry Clay Folger, who believed that a collation of as many texts as possible would reveal significant facts about the text of Shakespeare's plays. Dr. Charlton Hinman, using an ingenious machine of his own invention for mechanical collating, has made many discoveries that throw light on Shakespeare's text and on printing practices of the day.

The probability is that the First Folio of 1623 had an edition of between 1,000 and 1,250 copies. It is believed that it sold for £1, which made it an expensive book, for £1 in 1623 was equivalent to something between $40 and $50 in modern purchasing power.

During the seventeenth century, Shakespeare was sufficiently popular to warrant three later editions in folio size, the Second Folio of 1632, the Third Folio of 1663-1664, and the Fourth Folio of 1685. The Third Folio added six other plays ascribed to Shakespeare, but these are apocryphal.

THE SHAKESPEAREAN THEATRE

The theatres in which Shakespeare's plays were performed were vastly different from those we know today. The stage was a platform that jutted out into the area now occupied by the first rows of seats on the main floor, what is called the "orchestra" in America and the "pit" in England. This platform had no curtain to come down at the ends of acts and scenes. And although simple stage properties were available, the Elizabethan theatre lacked both the machinery and the elaborate movable scenery of the modern theatre. In the rear of the platform stage was a curtained area that could be used as an inner room, a tomb, or any such scene that might be required. A balcony above this inner room, and perhaps balconies on the sides of the stage, could represent the upper deck of a ship, the entry to Juliet's room, or a prison window. A trap door in the stage provided an entrance for ghosts and devils from the nether regions, and a similar trap in the canopied structure over the stage, known as the "heavens," made it possible to let down angels on a rope. These primitive stage arrangements help to account for many elements in Elizabethan plays. For example, since there was no curtain, the dramatist frequently felt the necessity of writing into his play action to clear the stage at the ends of acts and scenes. The funeral march at the end of *Hamlet* is not there merely for atmosphere; Shakespeare had to get the corpses off the stage. The lack of scenery also freed the dramatist from undue concern about the exact location of his sets, and the physical relation of his various settings to each other did not have to be worked out with the same precision as in the modern theatre.

Before London had buildings designed exclusively for theatrical entertainments, plays were given in inns and taverns. The characteristic inn of the period had an inner courtyard with rooms opening onto balconies overlooking the yard. Players could set up their temporary stages at one end of the yard and audiences could find seats on the balconies out of the weather. The poorer sort could stand or sit on the cobblestones in the yard, which was open to the sky. The first theatres followed this construction, and throughout the Elizabethan period the large public theatres had a yard in front of the stage open to the weather, with two or three tiers of covered balconies extending around the theatre. This physical structure again influenced the writing of plays. Because a dramatist wanted the actors to be heard, he frequently wrote into his play orations that could be delivered with declamatory effect. He also provided spectacle, buffoonery, and broad jests to keep the riotous groundlings in the yard entertained and quiet.

In another respect the Elizabethan theatre differed greatly from ours. It had no actresses. All women's roles were taken by boys, sometimes recruited from the boys' choirs of the London churches. Some of these youths acted their roles with great skill and the Elizabethans did not seem to be aware of any incongruity. The first actresses on the professional English stage appeared after the Restoration of Charles II, in 1660, when exiled Englishmen brought back from France practices of the French stage.

London in the Elizabethan period, as now, was the center of theatrical interest, though wandering actors from time to time traveled through the country performing in inns, halls, and the houses of the nobility. The first professional playhouse, called simply The Theatre, was erected by James Burbage, father of Shakespeare's colleague Richard Burbage, in 1576 on lands of the old Holywell Priory adjacent to Finsbury Fields, a playground and park area just north of the city walls. It had the advantage of being outside the city's jurisdiction and yet was near enough to be easily accessible. Soon after The Theatre was opened, another playhouse called The Curtain was erected in the same neighborhood. Both of these playhouses had open court-yards and were probably polygonal in shape.

About the time The Curtain opened, Richard Farrant, Master of the Children of the Chapel Royal at Windsor and of St. Paul's, conceived the idea of opening a "private" theatre in the old monastery buildings of the Blackfriars, not far from St. Paul's Cathedral in the heart of the city. This theatre was ostensibly to train the choirboys in plays for presentation at Court, but Farrant managed to present plays to paying audiences and achieved considerable success until aristocratic neighbors complained and had the theatre closed. This first Blackfriars Theatre was significant, however, because it popularized the boy actors in a professional way, and it paved the way for a second theatre in the Blackfriars, which Shakespeare's company took over more than thirty years later. By the last years of the sixteenth century, London had at least six professional theatres and still others were erected during the reign of James I.

The Globe Theatre, the playhouse that most people connect with Shakespeare, was erected early in 1599 on the Bankside, the area across the Thames from the city. Its construction had a dramatic beginning, for on the night of December 28, 1598, James Burbage's sons, Cuthbert and Richard, gathered together a crew who tore down the old theatre in Holywell and carted the timbers across the river to a site that they had chosen for a new playhouse. The reason for this clandestine operation was a row with the landowner over the lease to the Holywell property. The site chosen for the Globe was another playground outside of the city's jurisdiction, a region of somewhat unsavory character. Not far away was the Bear Garden, an amphitheatre devoted to the baiting of bears and bulls. This was also the region occupied by many houses of ill fame licensed by the Bishop of Winchester and the source of substantial revenue to him. But it was easily accessible either from London Bridge or by means of the cheap boats operated by the London watermen, and it had the great advantage of being beyond the authority of the Puritanical aldermen of London, who frowned on plays because they lured apprentices from work, filled their heads with improper ideas, and generally exerted a bad influence. The aldermen also complained that the crowds drawn together in the theatre helped to spread the plague.

The Globe was the handsomest theatre up to its time. It was a large building, apparently octagonal in shape and open like its predecessors to the sky in the center, but capable of seating a large audience in its covered balconies. To erect and operate the Globe, the Burbages organized a syndicate composed of the leading members of the dramatic company, of which Shakespeare was a member. Since it was open to the weather and depended on natural light, plays had to be given in the afternoon. This caused no hardship in the long afternoons of an English summer, but in the winter the weather was a great handicap and discouraged all except the hardiest. For that reason, in 1608 Shakespeare's company was glad to take over the lease of the second Blackfriars Theatre, a substantial roomy hall reconstructed within the framework of the old monastery building. This theatre was protected from the weather and its stage was artificially lighted by chandeliers of candles. This became the winter playhouse for Shakespeare's company and at once proved so popular that the congestion of traffic created an embarrassing problem. Stringent regulations had to be made for the movement of coaches in the vicinity. Shakespeare's company continued to use the Globe during the summer months. In 1613 a squib fired from a cannon during a performance of *Henry VIII* fell on the thatched roof and the Globe burned to the ground. The next year it was rebuilt.

London had other famous theatres. The Rose, just west of the Globe, was built by Philip Henslowe, a semi-literate denizen of the Bankside, who became one of the most important theatrical owners and producers of the Tudor and Stuart periods. What is more important for historians, he kept a detailed account book, which provides much of our information about theatrical history in his time. Another famous theatre on the Bankside was the Swan, which a Dutch priest, Johannes de Witt, visited in 1596. The crude drawing of the stage which he made was copied by his friend Arend van Buchell; it is one of the important pieces of contemporary evidence for theatrical construction. Among the other theatres, the Fortune, north of the city, on Golding Lane, and the Red Bull, even farther away from the city, off St. John's Street, were the most popular. The Red Bull, much frequented by apprentices, favored sensational and sometimes rowdy plays.

The actors who kept all of these theatres going were organized into companies under the protection of some noble patron. Traditionally actors had enjoyed a low reputation. In some of the ordinances they were classed as vagrants; in the phraseology of the time, "rogues, vagabonds, sturdy beggars, and common players" were all listed together as undesirables. To escape penalties often meted out to these characters, organized groups of actors managed to gain the protection of various personages of high degree. In the later years of Elizabeth's reign, a group flourished under the name of the Queen's Men; another group had the protection of the Lord Admiral and were known as the Lord Admiral's Men. Edward Alleyn, son-in-law of Philip Henslowe, was the leading spirit in the Lord Admiral's Men. Besides the adult companies, troupes of boy actors from time to time also enjoyed considerable popularity. Among these were the Children of Paul's and the Children of the Chapel Royal.

The company with which Shakespeare had a long association had for its first patron Henry Carey, Lord Hunsdon, the Lord Chamberlain, and hence they were known as the Lord Chamberlain's Men. After the accession of James I, they became the King's Men. This company was the great rival of the Lord Admiral's Men, managed by Henslowe and Alleyn.

All was not easy for the players in Shakespeare's time, for the aldermen of London were always eager for an excuse to close up the Blackfriars and any other theatres in their jurisdiction. The theatres outside the jurisdiction of London were not immune from interference, for they might be shut up by order of the Privy Council for meddling in politics or for various other offenses, or they might be closed in time of plague lest they spread infection. During plague times, the actors usually went on tour and played the provinces wherever they could find an audience. Particularly frightening were the plagues of 1592-1594 and 1613 when the theatres closed and the players, like many other Londoners, had to take to the country.

Though players had a low social status, they enjoyed great popularity, and one of the favorite forms of entertainment at Court was the performance of plays. To be commanded to perform at Court conferred great prestige upon a company of players, and printers frequently noted that fact when they published plays. Several of Shakespeare's plays were performed before the sovereign and Shakespeare himself undoubtedly acted in some of these plays.

REFERENCES FOR FURTHER READING

Many readers will want suggestions for further reading about Shakespeare and his times. The literature in this field is enormous but a few references will serve as guides to further study. A simple and useful little book is Gerald Sanders, *A Shakespeare Primer* (New York, 1950). *A Companion to Shakespeare Studies*, edited by Harley Granville-Barker and G. B. Harrison (Cambridge, Eng., 1934) is a valuable guide. More detailed but still not too voluminous to be confusing is Hazelton Spencer, *The Art and Life of William Shakespeare* (New York, 1940) which, like Sanders' handbook, contains a brief annotated list of useful books on various aspects of the subject. The most detailed and scholarly work providing complete factual information about Shakespeare is Sir Edmund Chambers, *William Shakespeare: A Study of Facts and Problems* (2 vols., Oxford, 1930). F. E. Halliday, *The Cult of Shakespeare* (London, 1957) presents an amusing and readable study of the ups and downs of Shakespeare's reputation with scholars, critics, actors, and the general public. For detailed, factual information about the Elizabethan and seventeenth-century stages, the definitive reference works are Sir Edmund Chambers, *The Elizabethan*

Stage (4 vols., Oxford, 1923) and Gerald E. Bentley, *The Jacobean and Caroline Stage* (5 vols., Oxford, 1941-1956). Alfred Harbage, *Shakespeare's Audience* (New York, 1941) throws light on the nature and tastes of the customers for whom Elizabethan dramatists wrote.

Although specialists disagree about details of stage construction, the reader will find essential information in John C. Adams, *The Globe Playhouse: Its Design and Equipment* (Barnes & Noble, 1961). A model of the Globe playhouse by Dr. Adams is on permanent exhibition in the Folger Shakespeare Library in Washington, D.C. An excellent description of the Globe is Irwin Smith, *Shakespeare's Globe Playhouse: A Modern Reconstruction in Text and Scale Drawings Based upon the Reconstruction of the Globe by John Canford Adams* (New York, 1956). Another recent study of the physical characteristics of the Globe is C. Walter Hodges, *The Globe Restored* (London, 1953). An easily read history of the early theatres is J. Q. Adams, *Shakespearean Playhouses: A History of English Theatres from the Beginnings to the Restoration* (Boston, 1917).

The following titles on theatrical history will provide information about Shakespeare's plays in later periods: Alfred Harbage, *Theatre for Shakespeare* (Toronto, 1955); Esther Cloudman Dunn, *Shakespeare in America* (New York, 1939); George C. D. Odell, *Shakespeare from Betterton to Irving* (2 vols., London, 1921); Arthur Colby Sprague, *Shakespeare and the Actors: The Stage Business in His Plays (1660-1905)* (Cambridge, Mass., 1944) and *Shakespearian Players and Performances* (Cambridge, Mass., 1953); Leslie Hotson, *The Commonwealth and Restoration Stage* (Cambridge, Mass., 1928); Alwin Thaler, *Shakespere to Sheridan: A*

Book About the Theatre of Yesterday and To-day
(Cambridge, Mass., 1922); Ernest Bradlee Watson,
*Sheridan to Robertson: A Study of the 19th-Century
London Stage* (Cambridge, Mass., 1926).

Enid Welsford, *The Court Masque* (Cambridge,
Eng., 1927) is an excellent study of the characteristics
of this form of entertainment.

Harley Granville-Barker, *Prefaces to Shakespeare* (5
vols., London, 1927-1948) provides stimulating critical
discussion of the plays. An older classic of criticism is
Andrew C. Bradley, *Shakespearean Tragedy: Lectures
on Hamlet, Othello, King Lear, Macbeth* (London,
1904), which is now available in an inexpensive reprint
(New York, 1955). Thomas M. Parrott, *Shakespearean
Comedy* (New York, 1949) is scholarly and readable.
Shakespeare's dramatizations of English history are
examined by E. M. W. Tillyard, *Shakespeare's History
Plays* (London, 1948), and Lily Bess Campbell, *Shakespeare's "Histories," Mirrors of Elizabethan Policy* (San
Marino, Calif., 1947) contains a more technical discussion of the same subject.

Interesting pictures as well as new information about
Shakespeare will be found in F. E. Halliday, *Shakespeare, a Pictorial Biography* (London, 1956). Allardyce
Nicoll, *The Elizabethans* (Cambridge, Eng., 1957) contains a variety of illustrations for the period.

A detailed and scholarly study of particular value in
understanding Shakespeare's approach to Roman history
is M. W. McCallum, *Shakespeare's Roman Plays and
Their Background* (London, 1910). An analysis of the
literature on this subject will be found in J. C. Maxwell,
"Shakespeare's Roman Plays, 1900-1956," in *Shakespeare Survey X* (Cambridge, Eng., 1957), pp. 1-11. In

the same publication is another useful essay, T. J. B. Spencer, "Shakespeare and the Elizabethan Romans," pp. 27-38. Sir Thomas North's translation of Plutarch, particularly the lives of Cæsar, Brutus, and Antony should be read in connection with the play. Various editions are available in libraries. The only recent edition of North's translation is one prepared for the Heritage Club by Roland Baughman (New York, 1955). Dryden's translation, however, has been reprinted in both the Modern Library and Everyman series. Neil S. Snodgrass, *Plutarch and Shakespeare* (New York, n.d.) gives a selection of the lives of Romans used by Shakespeare for his Roman plays.

A brief, clear, and accurate account of Tudor history is S. T. Bindoff, *The Tudors*, in the Penguin series. A readable general history is G. M. Trevelyan, *The History of England*, first published in 1926 and available in many editions. G. M. Trevelyan, *English Social History*, first published in 1942 and also available in many editions, provides fascinating information about England in all periods. Sir John Neale, *Queen Elizabeth* (London, 1934) is the best study of the great Queen. Various aspects of life in the Elizabethan period are treated in Louis B. Wright, *Middle-Class Culture in Elizabethan England* (Chapel Hill, N.C., 1935). *Shakespeare's England: An Account of the Life and Manners of His Age*, edited by Sidney Lee and C. T. Onions (2 vols., Oxford, 1916; new ed., 1952) provides a large amount of information on many aspects of life in the Elizabethan period. Additional information will be found in Muriel St. C. Byrne, *Elizabethan Life in Town and Country* (Barnes & Noble, 1961).

[Dramatis Personae

Julius Cæsar.

Octavius Cæsar, ⎫ Triumvirs
Marcus Antonius, ⎬ after the death
M. Æmilius Lepidus, ⎭ of Julius Cæsar.

Cicero, ⎫
Publius, ⎬ Senators.
Popilius Lena, ⎭

Marcus Brutus, ⎫
Cassius, ⎪
Casca, ⎪
Trebonius, ⎪ Conspirators against
Ligarius, ⎬ Julius Cæsar.
Decius Brutus, ⎪
Metellus Cimber, ⎪
Cinna, ⎭

Flavius and Marullus, Tribunes.

Artemidorus of Cnidos, a teacher of Rhetoric.

A Soothsayer.

Cinna, a poet.

Another Poet.

Lucilius, ⎫
Titinius, ⎪
Messala, ⎬ friends to Brutus and Cassius.
Young Cato, ⎪
Volumnius, ⎭

Dramatis Personae

Varro,
Clitus,
Claudius,
Strato, } servants to *Brutus.*
Lucius,
Dardanius,
Pindarus, servant to *Cassius.*
Calpurnia, wife to *Cæsar.*
Portia, wife to *Brutus.*
The Ghost of *Cæsar.*
Senators, Citizens, Guards, Attendants, Servants, &c.

Scene: *Rome; near Sardis; near Philippi.*]

THE TRAGEDY OF

JULIUS CÆSAR

ACT I

I.i. The Roman populace has turned out to celebrate the triumphant return of Julius Cæsar, but two of the tribunes, Flavius and Marullus, attempt to disperse the multitude because they fear that Cæsar's popularity may lead to the destruction of democracy in Rome.

▬▬▬▬▬▬▬▬▬

3. **Being mechanical:** being working people.

10. **in respect of:** compared with.

11. **cobbler:** botcher.

12. **directly:** frankly, without further punning.

15. **naughty:** good-for-nothing. The word often meant "wicked" and always had a stronger connotation than in modern usage.

ACT I

Scene I. [Rome. A street.]

*Enter Flavius, Marullus, and certain Commoners
over the stage.*

Flav. Hence! home, you idle creatures, get you home!
Is this a holiday? What, know you not,
Being mechanical, you ought not walk
Upon a laboring day without the sign
Of your profession? Speak, what trade art thou? 5

Car. Why, sir, a carpenter.

Mar. Where is thy leather apron and thy rule?
What dost thou with thy best apparel on?
You, sir, what trade are you?

Cob. Truly sir, in respect of a fine workman I am but, 10
as you would say, a cobbler.

Mar. But what trade art thou? Answer me directly.

Cob. A trade, sir, that I hope I may use with a safe
conscience, which is indeed, sir, a mender of bad soles.

Mar. What trade, thou knave? Thou naughty knave, 15
    what trade?

Cob. Nay, I beseech you, sir, be not out with me. Yet if
you be out, sir, I can mend you.

I

23. **awl:** an indispensable tool of the cobbler's trade.

26. **proper:** either "handsome" or "manly" may be meant.

27. **neat's leather:** cowhide.

49. **replication:** echo.

Cæsar embarking for Spain.

From *Commentarii di Caio Giulio Cesare* (1530).

Mar. What mean'st thou by that? Mend me, thou saucy
   fellow?   20

Cob. Why, sir, cobble you.

Flav. Thou art a cobbler, art thou?

Cob. Truly, sir, all that I live by is with the awl. I
meddle with no tradesman's matters nor women's matters,
but with all. I am indeed, sir, a surgeon to old shoes.   25
When they are in great danger, I recover them. As proper
men as ever trod upon neat's leather have gone upon my
handiwork.

Flav. But wherefore art not in thy shop today?
Why dost thou lead these men about the streets?   30

Cob. Truly, sir, to wear out their shoes, to get myself
into more work. But indeed, sir, we make holiday to see
Cæsar and to rejoice in his triumph.

Mar. Wherefore rejoice? What conquest brings he
   home?   35
What tributaries follow him to Rome
To grace in captive bonds his chariot wheels?
You blocks, you stones, you worse than senseless things!
O you hard hearts, you cruel men of Rome!
Knew you not Pompey? Many a time and oft   40
Have you climbed up to walls and battlements,
To tow'rs and windows, yea, to chimney tops,
Your infants in your arms, and there have sat
The livelong day, with patient expectation,
To see great Pompey pass the streets of Rome.   45
And when you saw his chariot but appear,
Have you not made an universal shout,
That Tiber trembled underneath her banks
To hear the replication of your sounds
Made in her concave shores?   50

52. **cull out a holiday:** choose a holiday from among ordinary workdays.

54. **Pompey's blood:** the kin of Pompey. Cæsar defeated Pompey's two sons in Spain.

57. **intermit:** delay.

61. **Tiber banks:** Shakespeare often uses a proper name as an adjective.

63. **the most exalted shores of all:** that is, the highest point on its banks to which the river ever rises.

64. **whe'r:** whether; a common elision; **their basest metal:** the most worthless nature among them.

68. **ceremonies:** symbols of religious observance. These are identified as scarves at I. [ii.] 290.

70. **the feast of Lupercal:** an annual festival, the Lupercalia, in honor of Lupercus (the god Pan).

And do you now put on your best attire?
And do you now cull out a holiday?
And do you now strew flowers in his way
That comes in triumph over Pompey's blood?
Be gone!   55
Run to your houses, fall upon your knees,
Pray to the gods to intermit the plague
That needs must light on this ingratitude.
   Flav. Go, go, good countrymen, and for this fault
Assemble all the poor men of your sort;   60
Draw them to Tiber banks, and weep your tears
Into the channel, till the lowest stream
Do kiss the most exalted shores of all.
                     Exeunt all the Commoners.
See, whe'r their basest metal be not moved.
They vanish tongue-tied in their guiltiness.   65
Go you down that way towards the Capitol;
This way will I. Disrobe the images
If you do find them decked with ceremonies.
   Mar. May we do so?
You know it is the feast of Lupercal.   70
   Flav. It is no matter. Let no images
Be hung with Cæsar's trophies. I'll about
And drive away the vulgar from the streets.
So do you too, where you perceive them thick.
These growing feathers plucked from Cæsar's wing   75
Will make him fly an ordinary pitch,
Who else would soar above the view of men
And keep us all in servile fearfulness.
                         Exeunt.

I. [ii.] Cæsar attends the race traditionally run on the Feast of Lupercal. A soothsayer warns him to beware of the ides of March. Cassius, a close friend of Brutus, sounds him out on the subject of Cæsar's growing power and Casca describes to them how Mark Antony three times offered Cæsar a crown, which he refused, although with greater reluctance each time. Brutus and Cassius agree to meet the next day and the latter is encouraged to think that Brutus may be stirred to action hostile to Cæsar.

Stage Dir. **Flourish**: a trumpet fanfare.

PROMPTV. ICONVM

Julius Cæsar.
From *Promptuarii iconum* (1553).

4

[Scene II. The same. A public place.]

[*Flourish.*] Enter *Cæsar*, *Antony* (for the course), *Calpurnia*, *Portia*, *Decius*, *Cicero*, *Brutus*, *Cassius*, *Casca*, [a great crowd following, among them,] a *Soothsayer*; after them, *Marullus* and *Flavius*.

Cæs. Calpurnia.
Casca.   Peace, ho! Cæsar speaks.
Cæs.   Calpurnia.
Cal. Here, my lord.
Cæs. Stand you directly in Antonius' way   5
When he doth run his course. Antonius.
Ant. Cæsar, my lord?
Cæs. Forget not in your speed, Antonius,
To touch Calpurnia; for our elders say
The barren, touched in this holy chase,   10
Shake off their sterile curse.
Ant.   I shall remember.
When Cæsar says "Do this," it is performed.
Cæs. Set on, and leave no ceremony out.
Sooth. Cæsar!   15
Cæs. Ha! Who calls?
Casca. Bid every noise be still. Peace yet again!
Cæs. Who is it in the press that calls on me?
I hear a tongue shriller than all the music
Cry "Cæsar!" Speak. Cæsar is turned to hear.   20
Sooth. Beware the ides of March.
Cæs.   What man is that?

Stage Dir. before 29. **Sennet:** the sounding of a trumpet.

29. **the order of the course:** what happens in the race.

38. **as I was wont to:** as I used to.

39. **stubborn:** harsh.

42-4. **If I have veiled my look,/ I turn the trouble of my countenance/ Merely upon myself:** if my manner is less frank, it is to keep entirely to myself the care that marks my face.

45. **passions of some difference:** conflicting emotions.

46. **Conceptions only proper to myself:** strictly personal thoughts.

47. **give some soil, perhaps, to my behaviors:** may mar the perfection of my manners to some degree.

50. **construe:** interpret.

Marcus Brutus.

From *Promptuarii iconum* (1553).

Bru. A soothsayer bids you beware the ides of March.
Cæs. Set him before me; let me see his face.
Cass. Fellow, come from the throng; look upon Cæsar.   25
Cæs. What say'st thou to me now? Speak once again.
Sooth. Beware the ides of March.
Cæs. He is a dreamer; let us leave him. Pass.
          Sennet. Exeunt. Manent Brutus and Cassius.
Cass. Will you go see the order of the course?
Bru. Not I.   30
Cass. I pray you do.
Bru. I am not gamesome. I do lack some part
Of that quick spirit that is in Antony.
Let me not hinder, Cassius, your desires.
I'll leave you.   35
Cass. Brutus, I do observe you now of late;
I have not from your eyes that gentleness
And show of love as I was wont to have.
You bear too stubborn and too strange a hand
Over your friend that loves you.   40
Bru.   Cassius,
Be not deceived. If I have veiled my look,
I turn the trouble of my countenance
Merely upon myself. Vexed I am
Of late with passions of some difference,   45
Conceptions only proper to myself,
Which give some soil, perhaps, to my behaviors;
But let not therefore my good friends be grieved
(Among which number, Cassius, be you one)
Nor construe any further my neglect   50
Than that poor Brutus, with himself at war,
Forgets the shows of love to other men.

53. **passion:** emotional state.

59. **just:** exact, true.

64. **respect:** reputation.

67. **had his eyes:** that is, that Brutus could see clearly.

76. **jealous:** suspicious; **on:** of.

77. **did use:** were [I] accustomed.

78. **stale:** cheapen by constant use.

81. **scandal:** slander.

82. **profess myself:** declare my affections.

83. **all the rout:** the whole company; **hold:** regard.

Cassius.

From *Promptuarii iconum* (1553).

Cass. Then, Brutus, I have much mistook your passion;
By means whereof this breast of mine hath buried
Thoughts of great value, worthy cogitations.　　55
Tell me, good Brutus, can you see your face?
Bru. No, Cassius, for the eye sees not itself
But by reflection, by some other things.
Cass. 'Tis just.
And it is very much lamented, Brutus,　　60
That you have no such mirrors as will turn
Your hidden worthiness into your eye,
That you might see your shadow. I have heard
Where many of the best respect in Rome
(Except immortal Cæsar), speaking of Brutus　　65
And groaning underneath this age's yoke,
Have wished that noble Brutus had his eyes.
Bru. Into what dangers would you lead me, Cassius,
That you would have me seek into myself
For that which is not in me?　　70
Cass. Therefore, good Brutus, be prepared to hear;
And since you know you cannot see yourself
So well as by reflection, I, your glass,
Will modestly discover to yourself
That of yourself which you yet know not of.　　75
And be not jealous on me, gentle Brutus.
Were I a common laugher, or did use
To stale with ordinary oaths my love
To every new protester; if you know
That I do fawn on men and hug them hard,　　80
And after scandal them; or if you know
That I profess myself in banqueting
To all the rout, then hold me dangerous.

94. **speed:** prosper.
97. **outward favor:** external appearance.
102. **such a thing as I myself:** i.e., another man.
111. **Accoutered:** equipped.

Flourish and shout.

Bru. What means this shouting? I do fear the people
Choose Cæsar for their king.   85
     Cass.   Ay, do you fear it?
Then must I think you would not have it so.
     Bru. I would not, Cassius, yet I love him well.
But wherefore do you hold me here so long?
What is it that you would impart to me?   90
If it be aught toward the general good,
Set honor in one eye and death i' the other,
And I will look on both indifferently;
For let the gods so speed me as I love
The name of honor more than I fear death.   95
     Cass. I know that virtue to be in you, Brutus,
As well as I do know your outward favor.
Well, honor is the subject of my story.
I cannot tell what you and other men
Think of this life, but for my single self,   100
I had as lief not be as live to be
In awe of such a thing as I myself.
I was born free as Cæsar, so were you;
We both have fed as well, and we can both
Endure the winter's cold as well as he.   105
For once, upon a raw and gusty day,
The troubled Tiber chafing with her shores,
Cæsar said to me, "Dar'st thou, Cassius, now
Leap in with me into this angry flood
And swim to yonder point?" Upon the word,   110
Accoutered as I was, I plunged in
And bade him follow. So indeed he did.

115. **hearts of controversy:** strong competitive spirits.

120. **Anchises:** the aged father of Æneas, the Virgilian hero and legendary founder of Rome.

129. **bend:** look.

130. **his:** its, referring to his eye.

136. **get the start of:** outdistance.

137. **palm:** prize.

Æneas bearing Anchises from the ruins of Troy.
From Andrea Alciati, *Emblematum* (1534).

The torrent roared, and we did buffet it
With lusty sinews, throwing it aside
And stemming it with hearts of controversy. 115
But ere we could arrive the point proposed,
Cæsar cried, "Help me, Cassius, or I sink!"
I, as Æneas, our great ancestor,
Did from the flames of Troy upon his shoulder
The old Anchises bear, so from the waves of Tiber 120
Did I the tired Cæsar. And this man
Is now become a god, and Cassius is
A wretched creature and must bend his body
If Cæsar carelessly but nod on him.
He had a fever when he was in Spain, 125
And when the fit was on him, I did mark
How he did shake. 'Tis true, this god did shake.
His coward lips did from their color fly,
And that same eye whose bend doth awe the world
Did lose his luster. I did hear him groan. 130
Ay, and that tongue of his that bade the Romans
Mark him and write his speeches in their books,
Alas, it cried, "Give me some drink, Titinius,"
As a sick girl! Ye gods, it doth amaze me
A man of such a feeble temper should 135
So get the start of the majestic world
And bear the palm alone.

Shout. Flourish.

Bru. Another general shout?
I do believe that these applauses are
For some new honors that are heaped on Cæsar. 140
    Cass. Why, man, he doth bestride the narrow world

142. **Colossus:** the statue of Apollo at Rhodes.

162. **Now is it Rome indeed, and room enough:** puns on **Rome** and **room**, which were pronounced similarly, were common. Since it is only big enough to hold one man, **Rome [room]** is an appropriate name for the city.

165. **a Brutus once:** Lucius Junius Brutus, claimed by Brutus as an ancestor, according to legend opposed Tarquin, last of the ancient kings of Rome; **brooked:** permitted.

168. **I am nothing jealous:** I have no doubt.

169. **aim:** guess.

An artist's conception of the Colossus of Rhodes as described by an early historian.
From André Thevet, *Cosmographie de Levant* (1554).

Like a Colossus, and we petty men
Walk under his huge legs and peep about
To find ourselves dishonorable graves.
Men at some time are masters of their fates.   145
The fault, dear Brutus, is not in our stars,
But in ourselves, that we are underlings.
"Brutus," and "Cæsar." What should be in that "Cæsar"?
Why should that name be sounded more than yours?
Write them together: yours is as fair a name.   150
Sound them: it doth become the mouth as well.
Weigh them: it is as heavy. Conjure with 'em:
"Brutus" will start a spirit as soon as "Cæsar."
Now in the names of all the gods at once,
Upon what meat doth this our Cæsar feed   155
That he is grown so great? Age, thou art shamed!
Rome, thou hast lost the breed of noble bloods!
When went there by an age since the great Flood
But it was famed with more than with one man?
When could they say (till now) that talked of Rome   160
That her wide walls encompassed but one man?
Now is it Rome indeed, and room enough,
When there is in it but one only man!
O, you and I have heard our fathers say
There was a Brutus once that would have brooked   165
The eternal devil to keep his state in Rome
As easily as a king.
     Bru. That you do love me I am nothing jealous.
What you would work me to, I have some aim.
How I have thought of this, and of these times,   170
I shall recount hereafter. For this present,
I would not (so with love I might entreat you)
Be any further moved. What you have said

176. **meet**: suitable.
181. **like**: likely.
191. **chidden**: scolded.
193. **ferret**: red like a ferret's eyes.
195. **crossed in conference**: frustrated in debate.

Cæsar witnessing military exercises by his men.

From *Commentarii di Caio Giulio Cesare* (1530).

I will consider; what you have to say
I will with patience hear, and find a time   175
Both meet to hear and answer such high things.
Till then, my noble friend, chew upon this:
Brutus had rather be a villager
Than to repute himself a son of Rome
Under these hard conditions as this time   180
Is like to lay upon us.
  Cass.   I am glad
That my weak words have struck but thus much show
Of fire from Brutus.

Enter Cæsar and his Train.

  Bru. The games are done, and Cæsar is returning.   185
  Cass. As they pass by, pluck Casca by the sleeve,
And he will (after his sour fashion) tell you
What hath proceeded worthy note today.
  Bru. I will do so. But look you, Cassius!
The angry spot doth glow on Cæsar's brow,   190
And all the rest look like a chidden train.
Calpurnia's cheek is pale, and Cicero
Looks with such ferret and such fiery eyes
As we have seen him in the Capitol,
Being crossed in conference by some senators.   195
  Cass. Casca will tell us what the matter is.
  Cæs. Antonius.
  Ant. Cæsar?
  Cæs. Let me have men about me that are fat,
Sleek-headed men, and such as sleep o' nights.   200
Yond Cassius has a lean and hungry look;

Coronets awarded to military victors.

From Claude Guichard, *Funerailles, & diverses manieres* (1581).
(See I. [ii.] 245.)

He thinks too much, such men are dangerous.

   Ant. Fear him not, Cæsar, he's not dangerous.
He is a noble Roman, and well given.

   Cæs. Would he were fatter! But I fear him not.   205
Yet if my name were liable to fear,
I do not know the man I should avoid
So soon as that spare Cassius. He reads much,
He is a great observer, and he looks
Quite through the deeds of men. He loves no plays   210
As thou dost, Antony; he hears no music.
Seldom he smiles, and smiles in such a sort
As if he mocked himself and scorned his spirit
That could be moved to smile at anything.
Such men as he be never at heart's ease   215
Whiles they behold a greater than themselves,
And therefore are they very dangerous.
I rather tell thee what is to be feared
Than what I fear; for always I am Cæsar.
Come on my right hand, for this ear is deaf,   220
And tell me truly what thou think'st of him.

           Sennet. Exeunt Cæsar and his Train.
                     [Manet Casca.]

   Casca. You pulled me by the cloak. Would you speak
    with me?

   Bru. Ay, Casca. Tell us what hath chanced today
That Cæsar looks so sad.   225

   Casca. Why, you were with him, were you not?

   Bru. I should not then ask Casca what had chanced.

   Casca. Why, there was a crown offered him; and being
offered him, he put it by with the back of his hand thus;
and then the people fell a-shouting.   230

   Bru. What was the second noise for?

246-47. **he would fain have had it:** he would have been pleased to have it; his refusal was not genuine.

252. **nightcaps:** such headgear was worn by all classes, but only the poorer folk wore theirs outside.

254. **swoonded:** swooned, fainted.

257. **soft:** hold, take it easy.

260. **falling sickness:** epilepsy.

Casca. Why, for that too.

Cass. They shouted thrice. What was the last cry for?

Casca. Why, for that too.

Bru. Was the crown offered him thrice? 235

Casca. Ay, marry, was't! and he put it by thrice, every time gentler than other; and at every putting-by mine honest neighbors shouted.

Cass. Who offered him the crown?

Casca. Why, Antony. 240

Bru. Tell us the manner of it, gentle Casca.

Casca. I can as well be hanged as tell the manner of it. It was mere foolery; I did not mark it. I saw Mark Antony offer him a crown—yet 'twas not a crown neither, 'twas one of these coronets—and, as I told you, he put it by 245 once; but for all that, to my thinking, he would fain have had it. Then he offered it to him again; then he put it by again; but to my thinking, he was very loath to lay his fingers off it. And then he offered it the third time. He put it the third time by; and still as he refused it, the rabble- 250 ment hooted, and clapped their chapped hands, and threw up their sweaty nightcaps, and uttered such a deal of stinking breath because Cæsar refused the crown that it had, almost, choked Cæsar; for he swoonded and fell down at it. And for mine own part, I durst not laugh, for 255 fear of opening my lips and receiving the bad air.

Cass. But soft, I pray you. What, did Cæsar swound?

Casca. He fell down in the market place and foamed at mouth and was speechless.

Bru. 'Tis very like. He hath the falling sickness. 260

Cass. No, Cæsar hath it not; but you, and I,
And honest Casca, we have the falling sickness.

Casca. I know not what you mean by that, but I am

271. **plucked me ope:** plucked open.

272. **An:** if; **a man of any occupation:** a crafts-man with a proper implement.

285. **To what effect:** what was the tenor of his words?

sure Cæsar fell down. If the tag-rag people did not clap
him and hiss him, according as he pleased and displeased 265
them, as they use to do the players in the theatre, I am no
true man.

Bru. What said he when he came unto himself?

Casca. Marry, before he fell down, when he perceived
the common herd was glad he refused the crown, he 270
plucked me ope his doublet and offered them his throat to
cut. An I had been a man of any occupation, if I would
not have taken him at a word I would I might go to hell
among the rogues. And so he fell. When he came to himself again, he said, if he had done or said anything amiss, 275
he desired their worships to think it was his infirmity.
Three or four wenches where I stood cried, "Alas, good
soul!" and forgave him with all their hearts. But there's no
heed to be taken of them. If Cæsar had stabbed their
mothers, they would have done no less. 280

Bru. And after that, he came thus sad away?

Casca. Ay.

Cass. Did Cicero say anything?

Casca. Ay, he spoke Greek.

Cass. To what effect? 285

Casca. Nay, an I tell you that, I'll ne'er look you i' the
face again. But those that understood him smiled at one
another and shook their heads; but for mine own part, it
was Greek to me. I could tell you more news too.
Marullus and Flavius, for pulling scarfs off Cæsar's 290
images, are put to silence. Fare you well. There was more
foolery yet, if I could remember it.

Cass. Will you sup with me tonight, Casca?

Casca. No, I am promised forth.

Cass. Will you dine with me tomorrow? 295

301. **quick mettle:** quick-witted.

304. **However:** even though; **puts on this tardy form:** adopts this slow-witted manner.

306. **disgest:** digest.

314-15. **wrought/ From that it is disposed:** worked so as to change it from its natural inclination.

316. **likes:** i.e., persons of similar nobility.

318. **bear me hard:** find me hard to tolerate.

325. **glanced at:** referred to by the way.

Casca. Ay, if I be alive, and your mind hold, and your
dinner worth eating.

Cass. Good. I will expect you.

Casca. Do so. Farewell both.   *Exit.*

Bru. What a blunt fellow is this grown to be!   300
He was quick mettle when he went to school.

Cass. So is he now in execution
Of any bold or noble enterprise,
However he puts on this tardy form.
This rudeness is a sauce to his good wit,   305
Which gives men stomach to disgest his words
With better appetite.

Bru. And so it is. For this time I will leave you.
Tomorrow, if you please to speak with me,
I will come home to you; or if you will,   310
Come home to me, and I will wait for you.

Cass. I will do so. Till then, think of the world.
                                    Exit Brutus.

Well, Brutus, thou art noble; yet I see
Thy honorable mettle may be wrought
From that it is disposed. Therefore it is meet   315
That noble minds keep ever with their likes;
For who so firm that cannot be seduced?
Cæsar doth bear me hard; but he loves Brutus.
If I were Brutus now and he were Cassius,
He should not humor me. I will this night,   320
In several hands, in at his windows throw,
As if they came from several citizens,
Writings, all tending to the great opinion
That Rome holds of his name; wherein obscurely
Cæsar's ambition shall be glanced at.   325

I. [iii.] Cassius speaks his mind to Casca and finds him disposed to join in a conspiracy to curb Cæsar. They meet Cinna, whom they send to "plant" a message designed to stir up Brutus. The conspirators are all to meet that night; Cassius and Casca also plan to call upon Brutus to seek his support.

　　　　　||||||||||||||||||||||||||||||||||||

18. **sensible:** aware.
19. **ha':** have.
21. **glared:** The Folios read "glazed," which is a dialect word of similar meaning and is retained by some editors.

And after this let Cæsar seat him sure,
For we will shake him, or worse days endure.

Exit.

[Scene III. The same. A street.]

Thunder and lightning. Enter, [from opposite sides,]
  Casca, [with his sword drawn,] and *Cicero.*

  Cic. Good even, Casca. Brought you Cæsar home?
Why are you breathless? and why stare you so?
  Casca. Are not you moved when all the sway of earth
Shakes like a thing unfirm? O Cicero,
I have seen tempests when the scolding winds   5
Have rived the knotty oaks, and I have seen
The ambitious ocean swell and rage and foam
To be exalted with the threat'ning clouds;
But never till tonight, never till now,
Did I go through a tempest dropping fire.   10
Either there is a civil strife in heaven,
Or else the world, too saucy with the gods,
Incenses them to send destruction.
  Cic. Why, saw you anything more wonderful?
  Casca. A common slave—you know him well by sight— 15
Held up his left hand, which did flame and burn
Like twenty torches joined; and yet his hand,
Not sensible of fire, remained unscorched.
Besides—I ha' not since put up my sword—
Against the Capitol I met a lion,   20
Who glared upon me, and went surly by

22-3. **drawn/ Upon a heap:** cowering closely together.

29. **conjointly meet:** occur simultaneously.

32. **climate:** clime, region.

35. **Clean from:** absolutely contrary to.

An omen in the sky.

From Julius Obsequens, *Prodigiorum liber* (1552).

Without annoying me. And there were drawn
Upon a heap a hundred ghastly women,
Transformed with their fear, who swore they saw
Men, all in fire, walk up and down the streets.   25
And yesterday the bird of night did sit
Even at noonday upon the market place,
Hooting and shrieking. When these prodigies
Do so conjointly meet, let not men say,
"These are their reasons, they are natural,"   30
For I believe they are portentous things
Unto the climate that they point upon.

Cic. Indeed it is a strange-disposed time.
But men may construe things after their fashion,
Clean from the purpose of the things themselves.   35
Comes Cæsar to the Capitol tomorrow?

Casca. He doth; for he did bid Antonius
Send word to you he would be there tomorrow.

Cic. Good night then, Casca. This disturbed sky
Is not to walk in.   40

Casca.   Farewell, Cicero.

Exit Cicero.

Enter *Cassius.*

Cass. Who's there?
Casca.   A Roman.
Cass.   Casca, by your voice.
Casca. Your ear is good. Cassius, what night is this!   45
Cass. A very pleasing night to honest men.
Casca. Who ever knew the heavens menace so?
Cass. Those that have known the earth so full of faults.
For my part, I have walked about the streets,
Submitting me unto the perilous night,   50

51. **unbraced:** unfastened. Cassius is pictured as wearing the typical Elizabethan doublet, which buttoned or laced down the front.

60. **astonish:** stun with awe and fear.

62. **want:** lack.

68. **birds and beasts, from quality and kind:** i.e., birds and beasts act unnaturally.

72. **monstrous:** greatly altered from the normal; exceedingly strange.

75. **monstrous:** abnormal, as in line 72.

And, thus unbraced, Casca, as you see,
Have bared my bosom to the thunder-stone;
And when the cross blue lightning seemed to open
The breast of heaven, I did present myself
Even in the aim and very flash of it.   55
  Casca. But wherefore did you so much tempt the
    heavens?
It is the part of men to fear and tremble
When the most mighty gods by tokens send
Such dreadful heralds to astonish us.   60
  Cass. You are dull, Casca, and those sparks of life
That should be in a Roman you do want,
Or else you use not. You look pale, and gaze,
And put on fear, and cast yourself in wonder,
To see the strange impatience of the heavens;   65
But if you would consider the true cause
Why all these fires, why all these gliding ghosts,
Why birds and beasts, from quality and kind;
Why old men fool and children calculate;
Why all these things change from their ordinance,   70
Their natures, and preformed faculties,
To monstrous quality, why, you shall find
That heaven hath infused them with these spirits
To make them instruments of fear and warning
Unto some monstrous state.   75
Now could I, Casca, name to thee a man
Most like this dreadful night
That thunders, lightens, opens graves, and roars
As doth the lion in the Capitol;
A man no mightier than thyself or me   80
In personal action, yet prodigious grown
And fearful, as these strange eruptions are.

85. **thews:** sinews.
86. **woe the while:** alas for these times.
88. **yoke and sufferance:** endurance of bondage.

A monument erected in honor of Cæsar near Constantinople.

From André Thevet, *Cosmographie de Levant* (1554).

Casca. 'Tis Cæsar that you mean. Is it not, Cassius?

Cass. Let it be who it is. For Romans now
Have thews and limbs like to their ancestors;   85
But woe the while! our fathers' minds are dead,
And we are governed with our mothers' spirits,
Our yoke and sufferance show us womanish.

Casca. Indeed, they say the senators tomorrow
Mean to establish Cæsar as a king,   90
And he shall wear his crown by sea and land
In every place save here in Italy.

Cass. I know where I will wear this dagger then;
Cassius from bondage will deliver Cassius.
Therein, ye gods, you make the weak most strong;   95
Therein, ye gods, you tyrants do defeat.
Nor stony tower, nor walls of beaten brass,
Nor airless dungeon, nor strong links of iron,
Can be retentive to the strength of spirit;
But life, being weary of these worldly bars,   100
Never lacks power to dismiss itself.
If I know this, know all the world besides,
That part of tyranny that I do bear
I can shake off at pleasure.   *Thunder still.*

Casca.   So can I.   105
So every bondman in his own hand bears
The power to cancel his captivity.

Cass. And why should Cæsar be a tyrant then?
Poor man! I know he would not be a wolf
But that he sees the Romans are but sheep;   110
He were no lion, were not Romans hinds.
Those that with haste will make a mighty fire
Begin it with weak straws. What trash is Rome,
What rubbish and what offal, when it serves

122. **fleering:** subserviently smiling.

123. **Be factious:** i.e., join the faction that is opposed to the evils we have been discussing.

132. **Pompey's Porch:** the entrance to Pompey's Theatre in the Campus Martius.

134. **complexion of the element:** disposition (nature) of the sky.

135. **favor:** appearance; see I. [ii.] 97.

137. **close:** concealed.

141. **incorporate:** joined in one body; i.e., as closely allied as possible.

142. **stayed for:** awaited.

143. **on't:** of it.

For the base matter to illuminate   115
So vile a thing as Cæsar! But, O grief,
Where hast thou led me? I, perhaps, speak this
Before a willing bondman. Then I know
My answer must be made. But I am armed,
And dangers are to me indifferent.   120
  Casca. You speak to Casca, and to such a man
That is no fleering telltale. Hold, my hand.
Be factious for redress of all these griefs,
And I will set this foot of mine as far
As who goes farthest.   125
  Cass.   There's a bargain made.
Now know you, Casca, I have moved already
Some certain of the noblest-minded Romans
To undergo with me an enterprise
Of honorable-dangerous consequence;   130
And I do know, by this they stay for me
In Pompey's Porch; for now, this fearful night,
There is no stir or walking in the streets,
And the complexion of the element
In favor's like the work we have in hand,   135
Most bloody, fiery, and most terrible.

Enter *Cinna.*

  Casca. Stand close awhile, for here comes one in haste.
  Cass. 'Tis Cinna. I do know him by his gait.
He is a friend. Cinna, where haste you so?
  Cin. To find out you. Who's that? Metellus Cimber?   140
  Cass. No, it is Casca, one incorporate
To our attempts. Am I not stayed for, Cinna?
  Cin. I am glad on't. What a fearful night is this!

149. **Be you content**: be satisfied; that is, you may be certain of that.

157. **hie**: hurry.

159. **repair**: betake yourself.

163. **yields him ours**: surrenders to us.

166. **countenance**: sanction; **like richest alchemy**: alchemists performed endless experiments to discover a method of changing base metals into gold. Casca believes that Brutus has so spotless a reputation that his participation in their plot will have the effect of ennobling their deeds.

169. **conceited**: thought out, interpreted.

There's two or three of us have seen strange sights.

   Cass. Am I not stayed for? Tell me.   145

   Cin.   Yes, you are.

O Cassius, if you could

But win the noble Brutus to our party—

   Cass. Be you content. Good Cinna, take this paper

And look you lay it in the prætor's chair,   150

Where Brutus may but find it, and throw this

In at his window. Set this up with wax

Upon old Brutus' statue. All this done,

Repair to Pompey's Porch, where you shall find us.

Is Decius Brutus and Trebonius there?   155

   Cin. All but Metellus Cimber, and he's gone

To seek you at your house. Well, I will hie

And so bestow these papers as you bade me.

   Cass. That done, repair to Pompey's Theatre.

                              Exit Cinna.

Come, Casca, you and I will yet ere day   160

See Brutus at his house. Three parts of him

Is ours already, and the man entire

Upon the next encounter yields him ours.

   Casca. O, he sits high in all the people's hearts,

And that which would appear offense in us,   165

His countenance, like richest alchemy,

Will change to virtue and to worthiness.

   Cass. Him and his worth and our great need of him

You have right well conceited. Let us go,

For it is after midnight, and ere day   170

We will awake him and be sure of him.

                                  Exeunt.

THE TRAGEDY OF

JULIUS CÆSAR

ACT II

II. [i.] Brutus, debating with himself the threat that Cæsar poses to the liberty of Rome, receives an anonymous letter from Cassius. Soon after, Cassius brings the conspirators to call upon him and they make a compact to assassinate Cæsar that very day.

⸻⸻⸻⸻⸻

11. **spurn:** oppose with hostility.

12. **the general:** i.e., the good of the citizenry in general; **He would be crowned:** he would like to be crowned.

ACT II

[Scene I. The same.]

Enter *Brutus* in his orchard.

Bru. What, Lucius, ho!
I cannot by the progress of the stars
Give guess how near to day. Lucius, I say!
I would it were my fault to sleep so soundly.
When, Lucius, when? Awake, I say! What, Lucius!   5

Enter *Lucius.*

Luc. Called you, my lord?
Bru. Get me a taper in my study, Lucius.
When it is lighted, come and call me here.
Luc. I will, my lord.   *Exit.*
Bru. It must be by his death; and for my part,   10
I know no personal cause to spurn at him,
But for the general. He would be crowned.
How that might change his nature, there's the question.
It is the bright day that brings forth the adder,
And that craves wary walking. Crown him that,   15
And then I grant we put a sting in him

21

20. **swayed:** weighed more heavily.

21. **a common proof:** a fact that has been confirmed by experience.

28-30. **since the quarrel/ Will bear no color for the thing he is,/ Fashion it thus:** since our case against him will not be supported by his known nature, this is how our case should be made.

33. **as his kind:** as is natural to his kind.

35. **closet:** private chamber.

40. **ides of March:** first of March in the First Folio; a correction suggested by Lewis Theobald.

That at his will he may do danger with.
The abuse of greatness is when it disjoins
Remorse from power. And to speak truth of Cæsar,
I have not known when his affections swayed   20
More than his reason. But 'tis a common proof
That lowliness is young ambition's ladder,
Whereto the climber-upward turns his face;
But when he once attains the upmost round,
He then unto the ladder turns his back,   25
Looks in the clouds, scorning the base degrees
By which he did ascend. So Cæsar may.
Then lest he may, prevent. And since the quarrel
Will bear no color for the thing he is,
Fashion it thus: that what he is, augmented,   30
Would run to these and these extremities;
And therefore think him as a serpent's egg,
Which, hatched, would as his kind grow mischievous,
And kill him in the shell.

Enter Lucius.

Luc. The taper burneth in your closet, sir.   35
Searching the window for a flint, I found
This paper, thus sealed up, and I am sure
It did not lie there when I went to bed.
                              Gives him the letter.
Bru. Get you to bed again; it is not day.
Is not tomorrow, boy, the ides of March?   40
Luc. I know not, sir.
Bru. Look in the calendar and bring me word.
Luc. I will, sir.   *Exit.*

44. **exhalations:** meteors.

51. **piece it out:** fill in mentally what is left unsaid.

64. **motion:** movement or gesture in that direction.

66. **genius:** inner self; **mortal instruments:** deadly agents; i.e., the impulses to deadly actions.

Bru. The exhalations, whizzing in the air,
Give so much light that I may read by them.   45
           Opens the letter and reads.

"Brutus, thou sleep'st. Awake, and see thyself!
Shall Rome, &c. Speak, strike, redress!"

"Brutus, thou sleep'st. Awake!"
Such instigations have been often dropped
Where I have took them up.   50
"Shall Rome, &c." Thus must I piece it out:
Shall Rome stand under one man's awe? What, Rome?
My ancestors did from the streets of Rome
The Tarquin drive when he was called a king.
"Speak, strike, redress!" Am I entreated   55
To speak and strike? O Rome, I make thee promise,
If the redress will follow, thou receivest
Thy full petition at the hand of Brutus!

           Enter *Lucius.*

Luc. Sir, March is wasted fifteen days.
           Knock within.
Bru. 'Tis good. Go to the gate, somebody knocks.   60
           [Exit Lucius.]
Since Cassius first did whet me against Cæsar,
I have not slept.
Between the acting of a dreadful thing
And the first motion, all the interim is
Like a phantasma or a hideous dream.   65
The genius and the mortal instruments
Are then in council, and the state of man,

73. **mo:** more; not a contraction of "more" but from a different root.

79. **any mark of favor:** any of their physical characteristics.

87. **For if thou path, thy native semblance on:** for if you continue in your normal way without disguise.

88. **Erebus:** the dark underground regions containing Hades.

Like to a little kingdom, suffers then
The nature of an insurrection.

Enter *Lucius.*

   Luc. Sir, 'tis your brother Cassius at the door,   70
Who doth desire to see you.
   Bru.   Is he alone?
   Luc. No, sir, there are mo with him.
   Bru.   Do you know
   them?   75
   Luc. No, sir. Their hats are plucked about their ears
And half their faces buried in their cloaks,
That by no means I may discover them
By any mark of favor.
   Bru.   Let 'em enter.   80
[Exit Lucius.]
They are the faction. O conspiracy,
Sham'st thou to show thy dang'rous brow by night,
When evils are most free? O, then by day
Where wilt thou find a cavern dark enough
To mask thy monstrous visage? Seek none, conspiracy,   85
Hide it in smiles and affability!
For if thou path, thy native semblance on,
Not Erebus itself were dim enough
To hide thee from prevention.

Enter the *Conspirators, Cassius, Casca, Decius, Cinna,*
Metellus [*Cimber*], and *Trebonius.*

   Cass. I think we are too bold upon your rest.   90

105. **watchful cares:** troubles that prevent sleep.

111. **fret:** intersect, as in ornamental patterns known as "fretwork."

114. **a great way growing on:** inclining considerably toward.

115. **Weighing:** considering.

121. **the face of men:** public opinion.

Good morrow, Brutus. Do we trouble you?
 Bru. I have been up this hour, awake all night.
Know I these men that come along with you?
 Cass. Yes, every man of them; and no man here
But honors you; and every one doth wish   95
You had but that opinion of yourself
Which every noble Roman bears of you.
This is Trebonius.
 Bru.   He is welcome hither.
 Cass. This, Decius Brutus.   100
 Bru.   He is welcome too.
 Cass. This, Casca; this, Cinna; and this, Metellus
    Cimber.
 Bru. They are all welcome.
What watchful cares do interpose themselves   105
Betwixt your eyes and night?
 Cass. Shall I entreat a word?

                                        They whisper.
 Dec. Here lies the east. Doth not the day break here?
 Casca. No.
 Cin. O, pardon, sir, it doth; and yon grey lines   110
That fret the clouds are messengers of day.
 Casca. You shall confess that you are both deceived.
Here, as I point my sword, the sun arises,
Which is a great way growing on the south,
Weighing the youthful season of the year.   115
Some two months hence, up higher toward the north
He first presents his fire; and the high east
Stands as the Capitol, directly here.
 Bru. Give me your hands all over, one by one.
 Cass. And let us swear our resolution.   120
 Bru. No, not an oath. If not the face of men,

122. **sufferance:** suffering; **the time's abuse:** the current abuses.

123. **betimes:** promptly.

125. **high-sighted:** haughty, overbearing.

126. **drop by lottery:** perish as his turn comes up; **these:** i.e., these motives.

131. **prick:** urge.

133. **palter:** equivocate, shilly-shally.

134. **honesty to honesty engaged:** honest men pledged to honorable action.

136. **cautelous:** crafty, overcautious; **men cautelous** therefore means men whose concern for their own safety makes them untrustworthy.

140. **even:** exact, unflawed.

141. **insuppressive:** irrepressible, invincible.

142. **or . . . or:** either . . . or.

ICONES.

MARCVS TVLLIVS CICERO PRI-
MVS PATER PATRIÆ.

Cicero.

From Jean de Tournes, *Insignium aliquot virorum icones* (1559).

The sufferance of our souls, the time's abuse—
If these be motives weak, break off betimes,
And every man hence to his idle bed.
So let high-sighted tyranny range on   125
Till each man drop by lottery. But if these
(As I am sure they do) bear fire enough
To kindle cowards and to steel with valor
The melting spirits of women, then, countrymen,
What need we any spur but our own cause   130
To prick us to redress? what other bond
Than secret Romans that have spoke the word
And will not palter? and what other oath
Than honesty to honesty engaged
That this shall be, or we will fall for it?   135
Swear priests and cowards and men cautelous,
Old feeble carrions and such suffering souls
That welcome wrongs; unto bad causes swear
Such creatures as men doubt; but do not stain
The even virtue of our enterprise,   140
Nor the insuppressive mettle of our spirits,
To think that or our cause or our performance
Did need an oath when every drop of blood
That every Roman bears, and nobly bears,
Is guilty of a several bastardy   145
If he do break the smallest particle
Of any promise that hath passed from him.
    Cass. But what of Cicero? Shall we sound him?
I think he will stand very strong with us.
    Casca. Let us not leave him out.   150
    Cin.   No, by no means.
    Met. O, let us have him! for his silver hairs
Will purchase us a good opinion

158. **break with him:** reveal our purpose to him.

164. **urged:** presented for consideration; **meet:** suitable; see I. [ii.] 176.

166. **of him:** in him.

167. **shrewd:** an adjective used to intensify meaning; here it indicates that Antony's plotting is not to be taken lightly.

168. **improve:** use, take advantage of.

169. **annoy:** injure.

173. **Like wrath in death and envy afterwards:** like killing in anger and then mutilating the remains from sheer malice.

178. **come by:** get at or influence.

And buy men's voices to commend our deeds.
It shall be said his judgment ruled our hands;   155
Our youths and wildness shall no whit appear,
But all be buried in his gravity.
  Bru. O, name him not! Let us not break with him,
For he will never follow anything
That other men begin.   160
  Cass.   Then leave him out.
  Casca. Indeed he is not fit.
  Dec. Shall no man else be touched but only Cæsar?
  Cass. Decius, well urged. I think it is not meet
Mark Antony, so well beloved of Cæsar,   165
Should outlive Cæsar. We shall find of him
A shrewd contriver; and you know, his means,
If he improve them, may well stretch so far
As to annoy us all; which to prevent,
Let Antony and Cæsar fall together.   170
  Bru. Our course will seem too bloody, Caius Cassius,
To cut the head off and then hack the limbs,
Like wrath in death and envy afterwards;
For Antony is but a limb of Cæsar.
Let us be sacrificers, but not butchers, Caius.   175
We all stand up against the spirit of Cæsar,
And in the spirit of men there is no blood.
O that we then could come by Cæsar's spirit
And not dismember Cæsar! But, alas,
Cæsar must bleed for it! And, gentle friends,   180
Let's kill him boldly, but not wrathfully;
Let's carve him as a dish fit for the gods,
Not hew him as a carcass fit for hounds.
And let our hearts, as subtle masters do,
Stir up their servants to an act of rage   185

187. **envious:** malicious; see **envy** at line 173.

194. **ingrafted:** deeply imbedded in his nature.

197. **take thought, and die:** grieve to death; **thought** was often used in the sense of "melancholy."

198. **that were much he should:** that's too much to expect of him.

200. **no fear:** nothing to be feared.

209. **main:** strong, positive.

210. **fantasy:** fancy; **ceremonies:** omens, which were often sought by prescribed religious rites.

211. **apparent prodigies:** conspicuous omens.

And after seem to chide 'em. This shall make
Our purpose necessary, and not envious;
Which so appearing to the common eyes,
We shall be called purgers, not murderers.
And for Mark Antony, think not of him;   190
For he can do no more than Cæsar's arm
When Cæsar's head is off.
    Cass.   Yet I fear him,
For in the ingrafted love he bears to Cæsar—
    Bru. Alas, good Cassius, do not think of him!   195
If he love Cæsar, all that he can do
Is to himself—take thought, and die for Cæsar.
And that were much he should; for he is given
To sports, to wildness, and much company.
    Treb. There is no fear in him. Let him not die,   200
For he will live and laugh at this hereafter.
                                Clock strikes.

    Bru. Peace! Count the clock.
    Cass.   The clock hath stricken
    three.
    Treb. 'Tis time to part.   205
    Cass.   But it is doubtful yet
Whether Cæsar will come forth today or no;
For he is superstitious grown of late,
Quite from the main opinion he held once
Of fantasy, of dreams, and ceremonies.   210
It may be these apparent prodigies,
The unaccustomed terror of this night,
And the persuasion of his augurers
May hold him from the Capitol today.
    Dec. Never fear that. If he be so resolved,   215
I can o'ersway him; for he loves to hear

217. **unicorns may be betrayed with trees**: the mythical unicorn could supposedly be caught by tricking it into running its horn into a tree.

218. **glasses**: mirrors; **holes**: camouflaged pits.

219. **toils**: nets.

223. **humor**: disposition, whim; **the true bent**: the very inclination that will suit us.

228. **doth bear Cæsar hard**: has a grievance against Cæsar; see I. [ii.] 318.

229. **rated**: berated, scolded.

231. **go along by him**: call upon him.

234. **upon's**: upon us.

239. **put on**: assume, don as a garment.

241. **formal constancy**: ordinary composure; **formal** has the sense of "normal" or "usual"; the conspirators are to behave as though nothing unusual were on their minds.

245. **fantasies**: fancies; see II. [i.] 210.

A unicorn.
From Conrad Gesner, *Historia animalium* (1587).

That unicorns may be betrayed with trees
And bears with glasses, elephants with holes,
Lions with toils, and men with flatterers;
But when I tell him he hates flatterers,   220
He says he does, being then most flattered.
Let me work,
For I can give his humor the true bent,
And I will bring him to the Capitol.
    Cass. Nay, we will all of us be there to fetch him.   225
    Bru. By the eighth hour. Is that the uttermost?
    Cin. Be that the uttermost, and fail not then.
    Met. Caius Ligarius doth bear Cæsar hard,
Who rated him for speaking well of Pompey.
I wonder none of you have thought of him.   230
    Bru. Now, good Metellus, go along by him.
He loves me well, and I have given him reasons.
Send him but hither, and I'll fashion him.
    Cass. The morning comes upon's. We'll leave you,
     Brutus.   235
And, friends, disperse yourselves; but all remember
What you have said and show yourselves true Romans.
    Bru. Good gentlemen, look fresh and merrily.
Let not our looks put on our purposes,
But bear it as our Roman actors do,   240
With untired spirits and formal constancy.
And so good morrow to you every one.
                       Exeunt. Manet Brutus.
Boy! Lucius! Fast asleep? It is no matter.
Enjoy the honey-heavy dew of slumber.
Thou hast no figures nor no fantasies   245
Which busy care draws in the brains of men;
Therefore thou sleep'st so sound.

250. **for your health**: i.e., healthy for you.

252. **ungently**: impolitely.

261. **wafture**: wave.

264. **withal**: in addition, at the same time.

265. **an effect of humor**: the result of a temporary mood or caprice; see II. [i.] 223.

269. **condition**: disposition.

270. **know you Brutus**: recognize you as Brutus.

276. **physical**: according to physic, i.e., medicine; wholesome.

277. **humors**: moistures, vapors.

Brutus' wife, Portia.

From *Promptuarii iconum* (1553).

Enter *Portia*.

Por.   Brutus, my lord!
    Bru. Portia! What mean you? Wherefore rise you now?
It is not for your health thus to commit   250
Your weak condition to the raw cold morning.
    Por. Nor for yours neither. Y' have ungently, Brutus,
Stole from my bed. And yesternight at supper
You suddenly arose and walked about,
Musing and sighing with your arms across;   255
And when I asked you what the matter was,
You stared upon me with ungentle looks.
I urged you further, then you scratched your head
And too impatiently stamped with your foot.
Yet I insisted, yet you answered not,   260
But with an angry wafture of your hand
Gave sign for me to leave you. So I did,
Fearing to strengthen that impatience
Which seemed too much enkindled, and withal
Hoping it was but an effect of humor,   265
Which sometime hath his hour with every man.
It will not let you eat nor talk nor sleep,
And could it work so much upon your shape
As it hath much prevailed on your condition,
I should not know you Brutus. Dear my lord,   270
Make me acquainted with your cause of grief.
    Bru. I am not well in health, and that is all.
    Por. Brutus is wise and, were he not in health,
He would embrace the means to come by it.
    Bru. Why, so I do. Good Portia, go to bed.   275
    Por. Is Brutus sick, and is it physical
To walk unbraced and suck up the humors

281. **rheumy**: damp; **unpurged**: unpurified.

283. **sick offense within your mind**: unnatural troubling of your mind.

286. **charm**: conjure.

288. **incorporate**: fuse into one body; see I. [iii.] 141.

290. **heavy**: grave, sorrowful.

299. **in sort or limitation**: in a way or with limitations.

Of the dank morning? What, is Brutus sick,
And will he steal out of his wholesome bed
To dare the vile contagion of the night,   280
And tempt the rheumy and unpurged air,
To add unto his sickness? No, my Brutus.
You have some sick offense within your mind,
Which by the right and virtue of my place
I ought to know of; and upon my knees   285
I charm you, by my once commended beauty,
By all your vows of love, and that great vow
Which did incorporate and make us one,
That you unfold to me, yourself, your half,
Why you are heavy, and what men tonight   290
Have had resort to you; for here have been
Some six or seven, who did hide their faces
Even from darkness.
   Bru.   Kneel not, gentle Portia.
   Por. I should not need if you were gentle Brutus.   295
Within the bond of marriage, tell me, Brutus,
Is it excepted I should know no secrets
That appertain to you? Am I yourself
But, as it were, in sort or limitation?
To keep with you at meals, comfort your bed,   300
And talk to you sometimes? Dwell I but in the suburbs
Of your good pleasure? If it be no more,
Portia is Brutus' harlot, not his wife.
   Bru. You are my true and honorable wife,
As dear to me as are the ruddy drops   305
That visit my sad heart.
   Por. If this were true, then should I know this secret.
I grant I am a woman, but withal
A woman that Lord Brutus took to wife.

315. **constancy:** fortitude; see II. [i.] 241.

324. **engagements:** undertakings.

325. **charactery:** symbolism, meaning.

330. **how:** how are you?

331. **Vouchsafe:** deign to accept.

333. **kerchief:** a cloth worn by women normally but by men and women alike to protect the head in time of sickness.

I grant I am a woman, but withal   310
A woman well-reputed, Cato's daughter.
Think you I am no stronger than my sex,
Being so fathered and so husbanded?
Tell me your counsels; I will not disclose 'em.
I have made strong proof of my constancy,   315
Giving myself a voluntary wound
Here, in the thigh. Can I bear that with patience,
And not my husband's secrets?
   Bru.   O ye gods,
Render me worthy of this noble wife!   *Knock.* 320
Hark, hark! one knocks. Portia, go in awhile,
And by-and-by thy bosom shall partake
The secrets of my heart.
All my engagements I will construe to thee,
All the charactery of my sad brows.   325
Leave me with haste.

                                         Exit Portia.
                 Lucius, who's that knocks?

             Enter *Lucius* and [*Caius*] *Ligarius.*

   Luc. Here is a sick man that would speak with you.
   Bru. Caius Ligarius, that Metellus spake of.
Boy, stand aside. Caius Ligarius, how?   330
   Caius. Vouchsafe good-morrow from a feeble tongue.
   Bru. O, what a time have you chose out, brave Caius,
To wear a kerchief! Would you were not sick!
   Caius. I am not sick if Brutus have in hand
Any exploit worthy the name of honor.   335
   Bru. Such an exploit have I in hand, Ligarius,

342. **mortified:** deadened, numbed.

⁂

II. [ii.] Cæsar's wife, Calpurnia, tries to prevent his going to the Capitol because of the many ill omens witnessed in Rome and finally persuades him to stay at home. But Decius Brutus, one of the conspirators, calls to escort Cæsar to the Capitol, convinces him that the omens are auspicious, and points out that he will appear ridiculous if he stays at home because of his wife's superstitions. The rest of the conspirators, headed by Brutus, enter to accompany Cæsar to the Capitol. As they are going, Mark Antony joins Cæsar's train.

⁂

Entrance. **nightgown:** a dressing gown, not a sleeping garment.

Had you a healthful ear to hear of it.

  Caius. By all the gods that Romans bow before,
I here discard my sickness! Soul of Rome!
Brave son, derived from honorable loins!   340
Thou like an exorcist hast conjured up
My mortified spirit. Now bid me run,
And I will strive with things impossible;
Yea, get the better of them. What's to do?

  Bru. A piece of work that will make sick men whole. 345

  Caius. But are not some whole that we must make sick?

  Bru. That must we also. What it is, my Caius,
I shall unfold to thee as we are going
To whom it must be done.

  Caius.   Set on your foot,   350
And with a heart new-fired I follow you,
To do I know not what; but it sufficeth
That Brutus leads me on.   *Thunder.*

  Bru.   Follow me then.

                                  Exeunt.

[Scene II. The same. Cæsar's house.]

Thunder and lightning. Enter *Julius Cæsar,*
in his nightgown.

  Cæs. Nor heaven nor earth have been at peace tonight.
Thrice hath Calpurnia in her sleep cried out
"Help, ho! They murder Cæsar!" Who's within?

5. **present**: immediate.

13. **stood on ceremonies**: took stock in omens; see II. [i.] 210.

20. **right form**: exact manner.

25. **beyond all use**: completely unusual, extraordinary.

Weapons of war as an omen in the sky.

From Julius Obsequens, *Prodigiorum liber* (1552).

Enter a *Servant.*

Serv. My lord?
Cæs. Go bid the priests do present sacrifice,   5
And bring me their opinions of success.
Serv. I will, my lord.   *Exit.*

Enter *Calpurnia.*

Cal. What mean you, Cæsar? Think you to walk forth?
You shall not stir out of your house today.
Cæs. Cæsar shall forth. The things that threatened me   10
Ne'er looked but on my back. When they shall see
The face of Cæsar, they are vanished.
Cal. Cæsar, I never stood on ceremonies,
Yet now they fright me. There is one within,
Besides the things that we have heard and seen,   15
Recounts most horrid sights seen by the watch.
A lioness hath whelped in the streets,
And graves have yawned and yielded up their dead.
Fierce fiery warriors fought upon the clouds
In ranks and squadrons and right form of war,   20
Which drizzled blood upon the Capitol.
The noise of battle hurtled in the air,
Horses did neigh, and dying men did groan,
And ghosts did shriek and squeal about the streets.
O Cæsar, these things are beyond all use,   25
And I do fear them!
Cæs.   What can be avoided
Whose end is purposed by the mighty gods?
Yet Cæsar shall go forth; for these predictions
Are to the world in general as to Cæsar.   30

59. **humor**: whim; see II. [i.] 223 and 265.

Cæsar's wife, Calpurnia.

From *Promptuarii iconum* (1553).

Cal. When beggars die there are no comets seen;
The heavens themselves blaze forth the death of princes.
  Cæs. Cowards die many times before their deaths;
The valiant never taste of death but once.
Of all the wonders that I yet have heard,   35
It seems to me most strange that men should fear,
Seeing that death, a necessary end,
Will come when it will come.

                    Enter a *Servant.*

                    What say the augurers?
  Serv. They would not have you to stir forth today.   40
Plucking the entrails of an offering forth,
They could not find a heart within the beast.
  Cæs. The gods do this in shame of cowardice.
Cæsar should be a beast without a heart
If he should stay at home today for fear.   45
No, Cæsar shall not. Danger knows full well
That Cæsar is more dangerous than he.
We are two lions littered in one day,
And I the elder and more terrible,
And Cæsar shall go forth.   50
  Cal.   Alas, my lord!
Your wisdom is consumed in confidence.
Do not go forth today. Call it my fear
That keeps you in the house and not your own.
We'll send Mark Antony to the Senate House,   55
And he shall say you are not well today.
Let me upon my knee prevail in this.
  Cæs. Mark Antony shall say I am not well,
And for thy humor I will stay at home.

63. **in very happy time:** very opportunely.
79. **stays:** holds.
80. **statuë:** trisyllabic.

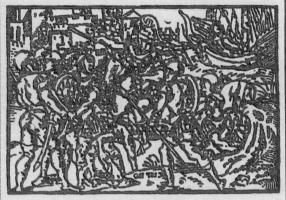

An episode of battle in the life of Cæsar.
From *Commentarii di Caio Giulio Cesare* (1530).

Enter *Decius.*

Here's Decius Brutus, he shall tell them so.   60
   Dec. Cæsar, all hail! Good morrow, worthy Cæsar!
I come to fetch you to the Senate House.
   Cæs. And you are come in very happy time
To bear my greeting to the senators
And tell them that I will not come today.   65
Cannot, is false; and that I dare not, falser:
I will not come today. Tell them so, Decius.
   Cal. Say he is sick.
   Cæs.   Shall Cæsar send a lie?
Have I in conquest stretched mine arm so far   70
To be afeard to tell greybeards the truth?
Decius, go tell them Cæsar will not come.
   Dec. Most mighty Cæsar, let me know some cause,
Lest I be laughed at when I tell them so.
   Cæs. The cause is in my will: I will not come.   75
That is enough to satisfy the Senate;
But for your private satisfaction,
Because I love you, I will let you know.
Calpurnia here, my wife, stays me at home.
She dreamt tonight she saw my statuë,   80
Which, like a fountain with an hundred spouts,
Did run pure blood, and many lusty Romans
Came smiling and did bathe their hands in it.
And these does she apply for warnings and portents
And evils imminent, and on her knee   85
Hath begged that I will stay at home today.
   Dec. This dream is all amiss interpreted;
It was a vision fair and fortunate.
Your statue spouting blood in many pipes,

93. **tinctures:** tints; i.e., synonymous with **stains;** **cognizance:** a term from heraldry; a badge worn to distinguish the retainers of a noble house.

100. **were:** would be.

101. **Apt:** ready at hand; **rendered:** given in return, responded.

107. **proceeding:** advancement.

108. **reason to my love is liable:** my love for you rules my judgment.

117. **Cæsar was ne'er so much your enemy:** Plutarch relates that Ligarius was pardoned by Cæsar when others accused him of being an ally of Pompey, but that Ligarius resented Cæsar's having the power to do him harm.

In which so many smiling Romans bathed,   90
Signifies that from you great Rome shall suck
Reviving blood, and that great men shall press
For tinctures, stains, relics, and cognizance.
This by Calpurnia's dream is signified.
    Cæs. And this way have you well expounded it.   95
    Dec. I have, when you have heard what I can say:
And know it now, the Senate have concluded
To give this day a crown to mighty Cæsar.
If you shall send them word you will not come,
Their minds may change. Besides, it were a mock   100
Apt to be rendered, for some one to say
"Break up the Senate till another time,
When Cæsar's wife shall meet with better dreams."
If Cæsar hide himself, shall they not whisper
"Lo, Cæsar is afraid"?   105
Pardon me, Cæsar, for my dear dear love
To your proceeding bids me tell you this,
And reason to my love is liable.
    Cæs. How foolish do your fears seem now, Calpurnia!
I am ashamed I did yield to them.   110
Give me my robe, for I will go.

    Enter *Brutus, Ligarius, Metellus, Casca, Trebonius,*
             Cinna, and *Publius.*

And look where Publius is come to fetch me.
    Pub. Good morrow, Cæsar.
    Cæs.   Welcome, Publius.
What, Brutus, are you stirred so early too?   115
Good morrow, Casca. Caius Ligarius,
Cæsar was ne'er so much your enemy

135. **That every like is not the same:** i.e., that some who seem like friends bear secret hostility.

136. **earns:** yearns, mourns.

<hr>

II. [iii.] Artemidorus, having learned of the conspiracy, writes a letter of warning to Cæsar and plans to hand it to him in the street before he reaches the Capitol.

As that same ague which hath made you lean.
What is't o'clock?
   Bru.   Cæsar, 'tis strucken eight.   120
   Cæs. I thank you for your pains and courtesy.

Enter *Antony*.

See! Antony, that revels long o' nights,
Is notwithstanding up. Good morrow, Antony.
   Ant. So to most noble Cæsar.
   Cæs.   Bid them prepare within. 125
I am to blame to be thus waited for.
Now, Cinna, now, Metellus. What, Trebonius!
I have an hour's talk in store for you;
Remember that you call on me today;
Be near me, that I may remember you.   130
   Treb. Cæsar, I will. [*Aside*] And so near will I be
That your best friends shall wish I had been further.
   Cæs. Good friends, go in and taste some wine with me,
And we (like friends) will straightway go together.
   Bru. [*Aside*] That every like is not the same, O Cæsar, 135
The heart of Brutus earns to think upon.
                           Exeunt.

[Scene III. The same. A street near the Capitol.]

Enter *Artemidorus*, [reading a paper].

   Art. "Cæsar, beware of Brutus; take heed of Cassius;
come not near Casca; have an eye to Cinna; trust not

7. **Security gives way to conspiracy:** inattention to danger opens the way for enemy plots.

14. **emulation:** envy.

16. **the Fates:** the three feminine deities who controlled human destiny.

━━━━━━━━━━━━━━━━━━━━━━━━━━━━━━━━

II. [iv.] Portia, Brutus' wife, who knows of the plot, nervously awaits word of its success. In the street she meets the soothsayer, who intends to warn Cæsar a second time, though he gives no indication of knowing the actual danger.

The three Fates.
From Vincenzo Cartari, *Imagini delli dei de gl'antichi* (1674).

39

Trebonius; mark well Metellus Cimber; Decius Brutus
loves thee not; thou hast wronged Caius Ligarius. There
is but one mind in all these men, and it is bent against   5
Cæsar. If thou beest not immortal, look about you.
Security gives way to conspiracy. The mighty gods defend
thee!

> "Thy lover,
>   "ARTEMIDORUS."   10

Here will I stand till Cæsar pass along
And as a suitor will I give him this.
My heart laments that virtue cannot live
Out of the teeth of emulation.
If thou read this, O Cæsar, thou mayst live;   15
If not, the Fates with traitors do contrive.

Exit.

[Scene IV. Before the house of Brutus.]

Enter *Portia* and *Lucius*.

Por. I prithee, boy, run to the Senate House.
Stay not to answer me, but get thee gone!
Why dost thou stay?
Luc.   To know my errand, madam.
Por. I would have had thee there and here again   5
Ere I can tell thee what thou shouldst do there.
O constancy, be strong upon my side,

21. **rumor**: uproar.
23. **Sooth**: truly.

Set a huge mountain 'tween my heart and tongue!
I have a man's mind, but a woman's might.
How hard it is for women to keep counsel!   10
Art thou here yet?
   Luc.   Madam, what should I do?
Run to the Capitol and nothing else?
And so return to you and nothing else?
   Por. Yes, bring me word, boy, if thy lord look well,   15
For he went sickly forth; and take good note
What Cæsar doth, what suitors press to him.
Hark, boy! What noise is that?
   Luc. I hear none, madam.
   Por.   Prithee, listen well.   20
I heard a bustling rumor like a fray,
And the wind brings it from the Capitol.
   Luc. Sooth, madam, I hear nothing.

Enter the *Soothsayer*.

   Por. Come hither, fellow. Which way hast thou been?
   Sooth. At mine own house, good lady.   25
   Por. What is't o'clock?
   Sooth.   About the ninth hour, lady.
   Por. Is Cæsar yet gone to the Capitol?
   Sooth. Madam, not yet. I go to take my stand,
To see him pass on to the Capitol.   30
   Por. Thou hast some suit to Cæsar, hast thou not?
   Sooth. That I have, lady. If it will please Cæsar
To be so good to Cæsar as to hear me,
I shall beseech him to befriend himself.
   Por. Why, know'st thou any harm's intended towards   35
    him?

41. **prætors**: elected magistrates.

51. **merry**: cheerful rather than gay as in modern usage.

   Sooth. None that I know will be, much that I fear may
     chance.
Good morrow to you. Here the street is narrow.
The throng that follows Cæsar at the heels,   40
Of senators, of prætors, common suitors,
Will crowd a feeble man almost to death.
I'll get me to a place more void and there
Speak to great Cæsar as he comes along.   *Exit.*

   Por. I must go in. Ay me, how weak a thing   45
The heart of woman is! O Brutus,
The heavens speed thee in thine enterprise—
Sure the boy heard me.—Brutus hath a suit
That Cæsar will not grant.—O, I grow faint.—
Run, Lucius, and commend me to my lord;   50
Say I am merry. Come to me again
And bring me word what he doth say to thee.
                             Exeunt [severally].

THE TRAGEDY OF

JULIUS CÆSAR

ACT III

III. [i.] Near the Capitol, Artemidorus attempts to urge his letter upon Cæsar, who refuses to give attention to it before other business and enters the Capitol. The conspirators crowd around Cæsar on a pretext and stab him to death. Brutus persuades them to leave Antony unharmed and proposes to explain their deed to the public and then to allow Antony to speak at Cæsar's funeral. Antony pretends friendly sympathy but privately resolves to avenge Cæsar's death with the help of Octavius Cæsar, whose presence in the vicinity is announced by a servant.

‖‖‖‖‖‖‖‖‖‖‖‖‖‖‖‖‖‖‖‖‖‖‖‖‖‖‖‖

3. **schedule**: note.

Stage Dir. after 13: Presumably the action shifts to a different part of the stage, perhaps to the upper stage.

ACT III

[Scene I. The same. A street in front of the Capitol.]

Flourish. Enter *Cæsar, Brutus, Cassius, Casca, Decius,*
  Metellus, Trebonius, Cinna, Antony, Lepidus,
  Artemidorus, [*Popilius,*] *Publius,* and the *Soothsayer.*

Cæs. The ides of March are come.
Sooth. Ay, Cæsar, but not gone.
Art. Hail, Cæsar! Read this schedule.
Dec. Trebonius doth desire you to o'erread
(At your best leisure) this his humble suit.   5
Art. O Cæsar, read mine first, for mine's a suit
That touches Cæsar nearer. Read it, great Cæsar!
Cæs. What touches us ourself shall be last served.
Art. Delay not, Cæsar! Read it instantly!
Cæs. What, is the fellow mad?   10
Pub.   Sirrah, give place.
Cass. What, urge you your petitions in the street?
Come to the Capitol.

[*Cæsar goes into the Senate House, the rest following.*]

42

20. **makes to:** behaves toward.

25. **constant:** unmoved, calm.

31. **prefer:** offer for consideration.

32. **addressed:** ready.

36. **puissant:** powerful.

42. **preordinance and first decree:** the ordinance existing already and the first decision laid down.

43. **the law of children:** that is, a decree which is easily reversed, as a child's mind is easily swayed; **fond:** foolish.

A Roman tribune.

From Pierre duChoul, *Discours de la religion des anciens Romains* (1556).

Pop. I wish your enterprise today may thrive.

Cass. What enterprise, Popilius? 15

Pop. Fare you well.

[*Advances to Cæsar.*]

Bru. What said Popilius Lena?

Cass. He wished today our enterprise might thrive.
I fear our purpose is discovered.

Bru. Look how he makes to Cæsar. Mark him. 20

Cass. Casca, be sudden, for we fear prevention.
Brutus, what shall be done? If this be known,
Cassius or Cæsar never shall turn back,
For I will slay myself.

Bru. Cassius, be constant. 25
Popilius Lena speaks not of our purposes,
For look, he smiles, and Cæsar doth not change.

Cass. Trebonius knows his time, for look you, Brutus,
He draws Mark Antony out of the way.

[*Exeunt Antony and Trebonius.*]

Dec. Where is Metellus Cimber? Let him go 30
And presently prefer his suit to Cæsar.

Bru. He is addressed. Press near and second him.

Cin. Casca, you are the first that rears your hand.

Cæs. Are we all ready? What is now amiss
That Cæsar and his Senate must redress? 35

Met. Most high, most mighty, and most puissant Cæsar,
Metellus Cimber throws before thy seat
An humble heart. [*Kneeling.*]

Cæs. I must prevent thee, Cimber.
These couchings and these lowly courtesies 40
Might fire the blood of ordinary men
And turn preordinance and first decree
Into the law of children. Be not fond

44. **rebel blood**: impulses which rebel against his reasoned decision.

51-2. **Cæsar doth not wrong, nor without cause/ Will he be satisfied**: Cæsar is never unjust and never punishes without cause. This is a passage which Ben Jonson, quoting inaccurately as "Cæsar did never wrong, but with just cause," ridiculed as nonsense in *Timber* in his own collected works (1641). It has been conjectured that the discrepancy between Jonson's quotation and the passage in the Folio indicates that Shakespeare altered the phraseology in the light of Jonson's ridicule, but it is equally possible that the latter remembered the passage incorrectly or misinterpreted it. There is no record of a printed version of the play before 1623 and Jonson may therefore have known it only in performance at the time his comment was written.

55. **repealing**: recall.

66. **resting**: remaining in one place.

72. **apprehensive**: susceptible to emotional influences.

74. **holds on his rank**: keeps straight ahead on his course.

To think that Cæsar bears such rebel blood
That will be thawed from the true quality   45
With that which melteth fools—I mean, sweet words,
Low-crooked curtsies, and base spaniel fawning.
Thy brother by decree is banished.
If thou dost bend and pray and fawn for him,
I spurn thee like a cur out of my way.   50
Know, Cæsar doth not wrong, nor without cause
Will he be satisfied.
    Met. Is there no voice more worthy than my own,
To sound more sweetly in great Cæsar's ear
For the repealing of my banished brother?   55
    Bru. I kiss thy hand, but not in flattery, Cæsar,
Desiring thee that Publius Cimber may
Have an immediate freedom of repeal.
    Cæs. What, Brutus?
    Cass.   Pardon, Cæsar! Cæsar, pardon!   60
As low as to thy foot doth Cassius fall
To beg enfranchisement for Publius Cimber.
    Cæs. I could be well moved, if I were as you;
If I could pray to move, prayers would move me:
But I am constant as the Northern Star,   65
Of whose true-fixed and resting quality
There is no fellow in the firmament.
The skies are painted with unnumb'red sparks,
They are all fire, and every one doth shine;
But there's but one in all doth hold his place.   70
So in the world: 'tis furnished well with men,
And men are flesh and blood, and apprehensive;
Yet in the number I do know but one
That unassailable holds on his rank,

75. **of**: by.
82. **bootless**: uselessly, vainly.
84. **Et tu, Brute**: and you, too, Brutus.
94. **confounded**: perplexed.
102. **abide**: suffer for.

Unshaked of motion; and that I am he,   75
Let me a little show it, even in this,
That I was constant Cimber should be banished
And constant do remain to keep him so.
   Cin. O Cæsar!
   Cæs.   Hence! Wilt thou lift up Olympus?   80
   Dec. Great Cæsar!
   Cæs.   Doth not Brutus bootless kneel?
   Casca. Speak hands for me!
                 They stab Cæsar [*—Casca, the others*
                          in turn, then Brutus].
   Cæs. Et tu, Brute?—Then fall Cæsar!   *Dies.*
   Cin. Liberty! Freedom! Tyranny is dead!   85
Run hence, proclaim, cry it about the streets!
   Cass. Some to the common pulpits and cry out
"Liberty, freedom, and enfranchisement!"
   Bru. People and Senators, be not affrighted.
Fly not; stand still. Ambition's debt is paid.   90
   Casca. Go to the pulpit, Brutus.
   Dec.   And Cassius too.
   Bru. Where's Publius?
   Cin. Here, quite confounded with this mutiny.
   Met. Stand fast together, lest some friend of Cæsar's   95
Should chance—
   Bru. Talk not of standing! Publius, good cheer.
There is no harm intended to your person
Nor to no Roman else. So tell them, Publius.
   Cass. And leave us, Publius, lest that the people,   100
Rushing on us, should do your age some mischief.
   Bru. Do so, and let no man abide this deed
But we the doers.

107. **As it were:** as if it were.

110. **stand upon:** care about.

124. **sport:** dramatic performance.

125. **basis:** pedestal; that is, the base of the statue of Pompey.

132. **grace:** dignify, do honor to.

Enter *Trebonius*.

Cass.   Where is Antony?

Treb. Fled to his house amazed.   105
Men, wives, and children stare, cry out, and run,
As it were doomsday.

Bru.   Fates, we will know your pleasures.
That we shall die, we know, 'tis but the time,
And drawing days out, that men stand upon.   110

Cass. Why, he that cuts off twenty years of life
Cuts off so many years of fearing death.

Bru. Grant that, and then is death a benefit.
So are we Cæsar's friends, that have abridged
His time of fearing death. Stoop, Romans, stoop,   115
And let us bathe our hands in Cæsar's blood
Up to the elbows and besmear our swords.
Then walk we forth, even to the market place,
And waving our red weapons o'er our heads,
Let's all cry, "Peace, freedom, and liberty!"   120

Cass. Stoop then and wash. How many ages hence
Shall this our lofty scene be acted over
In states unborn and accents yet unknown!

Bru. How many times shall Cæsar bleed in sport,
That now on Pompey's basis lies along   125
No worthier than the dust!

Cass.   So oft as that shall be,
So often shall the knot of us be called
The men that gave their country liberty.

Dec. What, shall we forth?   130

Cass.   Ay, every man away.
Brutus shall lead, and we will grace his heels
With the most boldest and best hearts of Rome.

134. **Soft:** just a moment, hold; see I. [ii.] 257.

138. **honest:** honorable.

143. **resolved:** answered, cleared of any doubt.

148. **Thorough:** through; **untrod state:** innovation in government.

152. **so please him:** if he pleases to.

155. **presently:** at once.

156. **well to friend:** well disposed to be friendly.

158. **still:** always.

159. **Falls:** turns out; **shrewdly:** grievously, to an extreme degree. The phrase means "My suspicions always prove distressingly accurate."

Enter a *Servant*.

Bru. Soft! who comes here? A friend of Antony's.
Serv. Thus, Brutus, did my master bid me kneel;   135
Thus did Mark Antony bid me fall down;
And being prostrate, thus he bade me say:
Brutus is noble, wise, valiant, and honest;
Cæsar was mighty, bold, royal, and loving.
Say I love Brutus and I honor him;   140
Say I feared Cæsar, honored him, and loved him.
If Brutus will vouchsafe that Antony
May safely come to him and be resolved
How Cæsar hath deserved to lie in death,
Mark Antony shall not love Cæsar dead   145
So well as Brutus living, but will follow
The fortunes and affairs of noble Brutus
Thorough the hazards of this untrod state
With all true faith. So says my master Antony.
Bru. Thy master is a wise and valiant Roman.   150
I never thought him worse.
Tell him, so please him come unto this place,
He shall be satisfied and, by my honor,
Depart untouched.
Serv.   I'll fetch him presently.   *Exit.* 155
Bru. I know that we shall have him well to friend.
Cass. I wish we may. But yet have I a mind
That fears him much; and my misgiving still
Falls shrewdly to the purpose.

Enter *Antony*.

Bru. But here comes Antony. Welcome, Mark Antony.   160

165. **rank:** suffering a corrupt condition, for which bloodletting was the conventional remedy.

171. **purpled:** bloodstained.

172. **Live:** that is, if I should live.

173. **apt:** ready; see II. [ii.] 101.

187. **Our arms in strength of malice:** both their arms, despite their show of strength in hostility to Cæsar, and their hearts, welcome Antony.

Mark Antony.
From Jean Baudoin, *Recueil d'emblemes divers* (1638-1639).

Ant. O mighty Cæsar! dost thou lie so low?
Are all thy conquests, glories, triumphs, spoils,
Shrunk to this little measure? Fare thee well.
I know not, gentlemen, what you intend,
Who else must be let blood, who else is rank.   165
If I myself, there is no hour so fit
As Cæsar's death's hour; nor no instrument
Of half that worth as those your swords, made rich
With the most noble blood of all this world.
I do beseech ye, if you bear me hard,   170
Now, whilst your purpled hands do reek and smoke,
Fulfil your pleasure. Live a thousand years,
I shall not find myself so apt to die;
No place will please me so, no mean of death,
As here by Cæsar, and by you cut off,   175
The choice and master spirits of this age.

Bru. O Antony, beg not your death of us!
Though now we must appear bloody and cruel,
As by our hands and this our present act
You see we do, yet see you but our hands   180
And this the bleeding business they have done.
Our hearts you see not. They are pitiful;
And pity to the general wrong of Rome
(As fire drives out fire, so pity pity)
Hath done this deed on Cæsar. For your part,   185
To you our swords have leaden points, Mark Antony.
Our arms in strength of malice, and our hearts
Of brothers' temper, do receive you in
With all kind love, good thoughts, and reverence.

Cass. Your voice shall be as strong as any man's   190
In the disposing of new dignities.

Bru. Only be patient till we have appeased

205. **credit:** reputation.

206. **conceit:** conceive; see I. [iii.] 169.

210. **dearer:** more intensely.

213. **corse:** corpse.

216-17. **close/ In terms of friendship:** come to friendly terms.

218. **bayed:** brought to bay; hunted to death.

220. **spoil:** ruin, destruction; **Signed in thy spoil:** marked (with blood) by the act of destroying you; **lethe:** lifeblood. **Lethe** was the name of the river in Hades which contained the waters of oblivion. The blood shed by Cæsar's murderers is pictured as equivalent to the waters of oblivion because his death is the result of the wounds.

The motto of Cesare Borgia: "Either Cæsar or nothing."
From Paulo Giovio, *Le sententiose imprese* (1588).

The multitude, beside themselves with fear,
And then we will deliver you the cause
Why I, that did love Cæsar when I struck him,   195
Have thus proceeded.
    Ant.   I doubt not of your wisdom.
Let each man render me his bloody hand.
First, Marcus Brutus, will I shake with you;
Next, Caius Cassius, do I take your hand;   200
Now, Decius Brutus, yours; now yours, Metellus;
Yours, Cinna; and, my valiant Casca, yours.
Though last, not least in love, yours, good Trebonius.
Gentlemen all—Alas, what shall I say?
My credit now stands on such slippery ground   205
That one of two bad ways you must conceit me,
Either a coward or a flatterer.
That I did love thee, Cæsar, O, 'tis true!
If then thy spirit look upon us now,
Shall it not grieve thee dearer than thy death   210
To see thy Antony making his peace,
Shaking the bloody fingers of thy foes,
Most noble! in the presence of thy corse?
Had I as many eyes as thou hast wounds,
Weeping as fast as they stream forth thy blood,   215
It would become me better than to close
In terms of friendship with thine enemies.
Pardon me, Julius! Here wast thou bayed, brave hart;
Here didst thou fall; and here thy hunters stand,
Signed in thy spoil, and crimsoned in thy lethe.   220
O world, thou wast the forest to this hart;
And this indeed, O world, the heart of thee!
How like a deer, strucken by many princes,
Dost thou here lie!

228. **cold modesty**: no more than a passionless understatement.

231. **pricked**: marked down on a list.

236. **Upon**: because of.

239. **good regard**: sound consideration.

246. **order**: course.

Cass. Mark Antony—   225
   Ant.   Pardon me, Caius Cassius.
The enemies of Cæsar shall say this;
Then, in a friend, it is cold modesty.
  Cass. I blame you not for praising Cæsar so;
But what compact mean you to have with us?   230
Will you be pricked in number of our friends,
Or shall we on, and not depend on you?
  Ant. Therefore I took your hands; but was indeed
Swayed from the point by looking down on Cæsar.
Friends am I with you all, and love you all,   235
Upon this hope, that you shall give me reasons
Why and wherein Cæsar was dangerous.
  Bru. Or else were this a savage spectacle.
Our reasons are so full of good regard
That were you, Antony, the son of Cæsar,   240
You should be satisfied.
  Ant.   That's all I seek;
And am moreover suitor that I may
Produce his body to the market place
And in the pulpit, as becomes a friend,   245
Speak in the order of his funeral.
  Bru. You shall, Mark Antony.
  Cass.   Brutus, a word with you.
[*Aside to Brutus*] You know not what you do. Do not
  consent   250
That Antony speak in his funeral.
Know you how much the people may be moved
By that which he will utter?
  Bru. [*Aside to Cassius*]   By your pardon,
I will myself into the pulpit first   255
And show the reason of our Cæsar's death.

262. **fall**: happen.
285. **cumber**: encumber, burden.

What Antony shall speak, I will protest
He speaks by leave and by permission,
And that we are contented Cæsar shall
Have all true rites and lawful ceremonies.   260
It shall advantage more than do us wrong.
    Cass. [*Aside to Brutus*] I know not what may fall. I
       like it not.
    Bru. Mark Antony, here, take you Cæsar's body.
You shall not in your funeral speech blame us,   265
But speak all good you can devise of Cæsar,
And say you do't by our permission.
Else shall you not have any hand at all
About his funeral. And you shall speak
In the same pulpit whereto I am going,   270
After my speech is ended.
    Ant.   Be it so.
I do desire no more.
    Bru. Prepare the body then, and follow us.
                      Exeunt. Manet Antony.
    Ant. O, pardon me, thou bleeding piece of earth,   275
That I am meek and gentle with these butchers!
Thou art the ruins of the noblest man
That ever lived in the tide of times.
Woe to the hand that shed this costly blood!
Over thy wounds now do I prophesy   280
(Which, like dumb mouths, do ope their ruby lips
To beg the voice and utterance of my tongue),
A curse shall light upon the limbs of men;
Domestic fury and fierce civil strife
Shall cumber all the parts of Italy;   285
Blood and destruction shall be so in use
And dreadful objects so familiar

290. **custom of fell deeds:** familiarity with cruelty.

292. **Ate:** the personification of discord and destruction.

294. **Havoc:** an old word to give the command for slaughter without quarter; **let slip:** release. A **slip** was a dog's leash.

313. **back:** i.e., come back.

316. **issue:** offspring, that which they have brought forth.

Horns of the Roman army.

From Pierre duChoul, *Discours de la religion des anciens Romains* (1556).

That mothers shall but smile when they behold
Their infants quartered with the hands of war,
All pity choked with custom of fell deeds;   290
And Cæsar's spirit, ranging for revenge,
With Ate by his side come hot from hell,
Shall in these confines with a monarch's voice
Cry "Havoc!" and let slip the dogs of war,
That this foul deed shall smell above the earth   295
With carrion men, groaning for burial.

                Enter *Octavius' Servant.*

You serve Octavius Cæsar, do you not?
    Serv. I do, Mark Antony.
    Ant. Cæsar did write for him to come to Rome.
    Serv. He did receive his letters and is coming,   300
And bid me say to you by word of mouth—
O Cæsar!
    Ant. Thy heart is big. Get thee apart and weep.
Passion, I see, is catching, for mine eyes,
Seeing those beads of sorrow stand in thine,   305
Began to water. Is thy master coming?
    Serv. He lies tonight within seven leagues of Rome.
    Ant. Post back with speed and tell him what hath
        chanced.
Here is a mourning Rome, a dangerous Rome,   310
No Rome of safety for Octavius yet.
Hie hence and tell him so. Yet stay awhile.
Thou shalt not back till I have borne this corse
Into the market place. There shall I try
In my oration how the people take   315
The cruel issue of these bloody men,

III. [ii.] Brutus tersely recites the reasons why Cæsar was a danger to the public good and the populace hail him as a hero. When Antony's turn comes, he cleverly works on the emotions of the mob; he reminds them of Cæsar's past benefactions, tells them that Cæsar has left all his wealth to the public, and stirs them to seek out and kill Cæsar's assassins. A servant informs Antony that Octavius has arrived in Rome and that Brutus and Cassius have ridden from the city.

━━━━━━━━━━━━━━━━━━━━━━━

11. **severally:** separately.
14. **lovers:** dear friends.
17. **Censure:** judge, weigh.

According to the which thou shalt discourse
To young Octavius of the state of things.
Lend me your hand.

Exeunt [with Cæsar's body].

[Scene II. The same. The Forum.]

Enter *Brutus* and *Cassius,* with the *Plebeians.*

Plebeians. We will be satisfied! Let us be satisfied!
Bru. Then follow me and give me audience, friends.
Cassius, go you into the other street
And part the numbers.
Those that will hear me speak, let 'em stay here;   5
Those that will follow Cassius, go with him;
And public reasons shall be rendered
Of Cæsar's death.
   1. Pleb.   I will hear Brutus speak.
   2. Pleb. I will hear Cassius, and compare their reasons   10
When severally we hear them rendered.
      [*Exit Cassius, with some of the Plebeians.*] *Brutus*
                              goes into the pulpit.
   3. Pleb. The noble Brutus is ascended. Silence!
   Bru. Be patient till the last.
Romans, countrymen, and lovers, hear me for my cause,
and be silent, that you may hear. Believe me for mine   15
honor, and have respect to mine honor, that you may believe. Censure me in your wisdom, and awake your
senses, that you may the better judge. If there be any in
this assembly, any dear friend of Cæsar's, to him I say

37. **the question of:** the whole story of.
38-9. **extenuated:** underrated, minimized.
39. **enforced:** exaggerated, overstated.

that Brutus' love to Cæsar was no less than his. If then　20
that friend demand why Brutus rose against Cæsar, this
is my answer: Not that I loved Cæsar less, but that I
loved Rome more. Had you rather Cæsar were living,
and die all slaves, than that Cæsar were dead, to live all
freemen? As Cæsar loved me, I weep for him; as he was　25
fortunate, I rejoice at it; as he was valiant, I honor him,
but—as he was ambitious, I slew him. There is tears for
his love; joy for his fortune; honor for his valor; and
death for his ambition. Who is here so base that would
be a bondman? If any, speak, for him have I offended.　30
Who is here so rude that would not be a Roman? If any,
speak, for him have I offended. Who is here so vile that
will not love his country? If any, speak, for him have I
offended. I pause for a reply.

All. None, Brutus, none!　35

Bru. Then none have I offended. I have done no more
to Cæsar than you shall do to Brutus. The questi)n of
his death is enrolled in the Capitol; his glory not extenuated, wherein he was worthy, nor his offenses enforced,
for which he suffered death　40

Enter *Mark Antony* [and others], with *Cæsar's* body.

Here comes his body, mourned by Mark Antony, who,
though he had no hand in his death, shall receive the
benefit of his dying, a place in the commonwealth, as
which of you shall not? With this I depart, that, as I slew
my best lover for the good of Rome, I have the same　45
dagger for myself when it shall please my country to
need my death.

All. Live, Brutus! live, live!

61. **grace**: honor; see III. [i.] 132.

1. Pleb. Bring him with triumph home unto his house.

2. Pleb. Give him a statue with his ancestors.   50

3. Pleb. Let him be Cæsar.

4. Pleb.   Cæsar's better parts
Shall be crowned in Brutus.

1. Pleb. We'll bring him to his house with shouts and
   clamors.   55

Bru. My countrymen—

2. Pleb.   Peace! silence! Brutus speaks.

1. Pleb. Peace, ho!

Bru. Good countrymen, let me depart alone,
And, for my sake, stay here with Antony.   60
Do grace to Cæsar's corpse, and grace his speech
Tending to Cæsar's glories which Mark Antony,
By our permission, is allowed to make.
I do entreat you, not a man depart,
Save I alone, till Antony have spoke.   *Exit.*   65

1. Pleb. Stay, ho! and let us hear Mark Antony.

3. Pleb. Let him go up into the public chair.
We'll hear him. Noble Antony, go up.

Ant. For Brutus' sake I am beholding to you.
                    [*Goes into the pulpit.*]

4. Pleb. What does he say of Brutus?   70

3. Pleb.   He says for Brutus' sake
He finds himself beholding to us all.

4. Pleb. 'Twere best he speak no harm of Brutus here!

1. Pleb. This Cæsar was a tyrant.

3. Pleb.   Nay, that's certain.   75
We are blest that Rome is rid of him.

2. Pleb. Peace! Let us hear what Antony can say.

Ant. You gentle Romans—

All.   Peace, ho! Let us hear him.

88. **under leave:** by permission.

102. **the Lupercal:** that is, the day of the Feast of Lupercal.

Ant. Friends, Romans, countrymen, lend me your ears;   80
I come to bury Cæsar, not to praise him.
The evil that men do lives after them;
The good is oft interred with their bones.
So let it be with Cæsar. The noble Brutus
Hath told you Cæsar was ambitious.   85
If it were so, it was a grievous fault,
And grievously hath Cæsar answered it.
Here, under leave of Brutus and the rest
(For Brutus is an honorable man;
So are they all, all honorable men),   90
Come I to speak in Cæsar's funeral.
He was my friend, faithful and just to me;
But Brutus says he was ambitious,
And Brutus is an honorable man.
He hath brought many captives home to Rome,   95
Whose ransoms did the general coffers fill.
Did this in Cæsar seem ambitious?
When that the poor have cried, Cæsar hath wept;
Ambition should be made of sterner stuff.
Yet Brutus says he was ambitious;   100
And Brutus is an honorable man.
You all did see that on the Lupercal
I thrice presented him a kingly crown,
Which he did thrice refuse. Was this ambition?
Yet Brutus says he was ambitious;   105
And sure he is an honorable man.
I speak not to disprove what Brutus spoke,
But here I am to speak what I do know.
You all did love him once, not without cause.
What cause withholds you then to mourn for him?   110
O judgment, thou art fled to brutish beasts,

119. **I fear there will a worse come in his place:** an echo of the proverb, "Seldom comes a better."

123. **dear abide:** pay dearly for; see III. [i.] 102.

141. **commons:** multitude.

And men have lost their reason! Bear with me,
My heart is in the coffin there with Cæsar,
And I must pause till it come back to me.

  1. Pleb. Methinks there is much reason in his sayings. 115

  2. Pleb. If thou consider rightly of the matter,
Cæsar has had great wrong.

  3. Pleb.   Has he, masters?
I fear there will a worse come in his place.

  4. Pleb. Marked ye his words? He would not take the 120
    crown;
Therefore 'tis certain he was not ambitious.

  1. Pleb. If it be found so, some will dear abide it.

  2. Pleb. Poor soul! his eyes are red as fire with weep-
    ing. 125

  3. Pleb. There's not a nobler man in Rome than
    Antony.

  4. Pleb. Now mark him. He begins again to speak.

  Ant. But yesterday the word of Cæsar might
Have stood against the world. Now lies he there, 130
And none so poor to do him reverence.
O masters! If I were disposed to stir
Your hearts and minds to mutiny and rage,
I should do Brutus wrong, and Cassius wrong,
Who, you all know, are honorable men. 135
I will not do them wrong. I rather choose
To wrong the dead, to wrong myself and you,
Than I will wrong such honorable men.
But here's a parchment with the seal of Cæsar.
I found it in his closet; 'tis his will. 140
Let but the commons hear this testament,
Which (pardon me) I do not mean to read,
And they would go and kiss dead Cæsar's wounds

144. **napkins**: handkerchiefs.

Cæsar's forces in the Gallic campaigns.

From *Commentarii di Caio Giulio Cesare* (1530).

And dip their napkins in his sacred blood;
Yea, beg a hair of him for memory, 145
And dying, mention it within their wills,
Bequeathing it as a rich legacy
Unto their issue.

  4. Pleb. We'll hear the will! Read it, Mark Antony.
  All. The will, the will! We will hear Cæsar's will! 150
  Ant. Have patience, gentle friends, I must not read it.
It is not meet you know how Cæsar loved you.
You are not wood, you are not stones, but men;
And being men, hearing the will of Cæsar,
It will inflame you, it will make you mad. 155
'Tis good you know not that you are his heirs,
For if you should, O, what would come of it?
  4. Pleb. Read the will! We'll hear it, Antony!
You shall read us the will, Cæsar's will!
  Ant. Will you be patient? Will you stay awhile? 160
I have o'ershot myself to tell you of it.
I fear I wrong the honorable men
Whose daggers have stabbed Cæsar; I do fear it.
  4. Pleb. They were traitors. Honorable men!
  All. The will! the testament! 165
  2. Pleb. They were villains, murderers! The will! Read
the will!
  Ant. You will compel me then to read the will?
Then make a ring about the corpse of Cæsar
And let me show you him that made the will. 170
Shall I descend? and will you give me leave?
  All. Come down.
  2. Pleb. Descend.
  3. Pleb. You shall have leave.

                            [*Antony comes down.*]

184. **the Nervii:** one of the tribes conquered by Cæsar in his campaigns in Gaul.

205. **dint:** dent, effect.

Roman soldiers.
From Pierre duChoul, *Discours de la religion des anciens Romains* (1556).

4. Pleb. A ring! Stand round.   175
1. Pleb. Stand from the hearse! Stand from the body!
2. Pleb. Room for Antony, most noble Antony!
Ant. Nay, press not so upon me. Stand far off.
All. Stand back! Room! Bear back!
Ant. If you have tears, prepare to shed them now.   180
You all do know this mantle. I remember
The first time ever Cæsar put it on.
'Twas on a summer's evening in his tent,
That day he overcame the Nervii.
Look, in this place ran Cassius' dagger through.   185
See what a rent the envious Casca made.
Through this the well-beloved Brutus stabbed;
And as he plucked his cursed steel away,
Mark how the blood of Cæsar followed it,
As rushing out of doors to be resolved   190
If Brutus so unkindly knocked or no;
For Brutus, as you know, was Cæsar's angel.
Judge, O you gods, how dearly Cæsar loved him!
This was the most unkindest cut of all;
For when the noble Cæsar saw him stab,   195
Ingratitude, more strong than traitors' arms,
Quite vanquished him. Then burst his mighty heart;
And in his mantle muffling up his face,
Even at the base of Pompey's statuë
(Which all the while ran blood) great Cæsar fell.   200
O, what a fall was there, my countrymen!
Then I, and you, and all of us fell down,
Whilst bloody treason flourished over us.
O, now you weep, and I perceive you feel
The dint of pity. These are gracious drops.   205
Kind souls, what, weep you when you but behold

207. **vesture:** clothing.
238. **there were:** then there would be.

Our Cæsar's vesture wounded? Look you here!
Here is himself, marred as you see with traitors.
  1. Pleb. O piteous spectacle!
  2. Pleb. O noble Cæsar!   210
  3. Pleb. O woeful day!
  4. Pleb. O traitors, villains!
  1. Pleb. O most bloody sight!
  2. Pleb. We will be revenged.
  All. Revenge! About! Seek! Burn! Fire! Kill! Slay! 215
Let not a traitor live!
  Ant. Stay, countrymen.
  1. Pleb. Peace there! Hear the noble Antony.
  2. Pleb. We'll hear him, we'll follow him, we'll die
with him!   220
  Ant. Good friends, sweet friends, let me not stir you up
To such a sudden flood of mutiny.
They that have done this deed are honorable.
What private griefs they have, alas, I know not,
That made them do it. They are wise and honorable,   225
And will no doubt with reasons answer you.
I come not, friends, to steal away your hearts.
I am no orator, as Brutus is,
But (as you know me all) a plain blunt man
That love my friend; and that they know full well   230
That gave me public leave to speak of him.
For I have neither wit, nor words, nor worth,
Action, nor utterance, nor the power of speech
To stir men's blood. I only speak right on.
I tell you that which you yourselves do know,   235
Show you sweet Cæsar's wounds, poor poor dumb mouths,
And bid them speak for me. But were I Brutus,
And Brutus Antony, there were an Antony

239. **ruffle**: stir violently.

Would ruffle up your spirits, and put a tongue
In every wound of Cæsar that should move   240
The stones of Rome to rise and mutiny.
   All. We'll mutiny.
   1. Pleb.   We'll burn the house of Brutus.
   3. Pleb. Away then! Come, seek the conspirators.
   Ant. Yet hear me, countrymen. Yet hear me speak.   245
   All. Peace, ho! Hear Antony, most noble Antony!
   Ant. Why, friends, you go to do you know not what.
Wherein hath Cæsar thus deserved your loves?
Alas, you know not! I must tell you then.
You have forgot the will I told you of.   250
   All. Most true! The will! Let's stay and hear the will.
   Ant. Here is the will, and under Cæsar's seal.
To every Roman citizen he gives,
To every several man, seventy-five drachmas.
   2. Pleb. Most noble Cæsar! We'll revenge his death!   255
   3. Pleb. O royal Cæsar!
   Ant. Hear me with patience.
   All. Peace, ho!
   Ant. Moreover, he hath left you all his walks,
His private arbors, and new-planted orchards,   260
On this side Tiber; he hath left them you,
And to your heirs for ever—common pleasures,
To walk abroad and recreate yourselves.
Here was a Cæsar! When comes such another?
   1. Pleb. Never, never! Come, away, away!   265
We'll burn his body in the holy place
And with the brands fire the traitors' houses.
Take up the body.
   2. Pleb. Go fetch fire!
   3. Pleb. Pluck down benches!   270

271. **forms:** benches.
278. **straight:** immediately.
283. **Belike:** most likely.

━━━━━━━━━━━━━━━━━━━━━━━━━━

III. [iii.] Cinna the poet is assailed by the mob and killed because he has the same name as one of the conspirators. Enraged, the mob then moves on to dispose of Cæsar's murderers.

━━━━━━━━━━━━━━━━━━━━━━

2. **things unluckily charge my fantasy:** bad omens burden my imagination.

4. *Pleb.* Pluck down forms, windows, anything!
                    Exeunt Plebeians [with the body].
  Ant. Now let it work. Mischief, thou art afoot,
Take thou what course thou wilt.

                    Enter *Servant.*

                        How now, fellow?
  Serv. Sir, Octavius is already come to Rome.   275
  Ant. Where is he?
  Serv. He and Lepidus are at Cæsar's house.
  Ant. And thither will I straight to visit him.
He comes upon a wish. Fortune is merry,
And in this mood will give us anything.   280
  Serv. I heard him say Brutus and Cassius
Are rid like madmen through the gates of Rome.
  Ant. Belike they had some notice of the people
How I had moved them. Bring me to Octavius.

                                        Exeunt.

[Scene III. The same. A street.]

Enter *Cinna* the *Poet*, and after him the *Plebeians.*

  Cin. I dreamt tonight that I did feast with Cæsar,
And things unluckily charge my fantasy.
I have no will to wander forth of doors,
Yet something leads me forth.
  1. Pleb. What is your name?   5
  2. Pleb. Whither are you going?

12. **you were best**: if you know what is good for you.

18. **bear me a bang**: get a blow from me.

3. Pleb. Where do you dwell?

4. Pleb. Are you a married man or a bachelor?

2. Pleb. Answer every man directly.

1. Pleb. Ay, and briefly.   10

4. Pleb. Ay, and wisely.

3. Pleb. Ay, and truly, you were best.

Cin. What is my name? Whither am I going? Where
do I dwell? Am I a married man or a bachelor? Then, to
answer every man directly and briefly, wisely and truly: 15
wisely I say, I am a bachelor.

2. Pleb. That's as much as to say they are fools that
marry. You'll bear me a bang for that, I fear. Proceed—
directly.

Cin. Directly I am going to Cæsar's funeral.   20

1. Pleb. As a friend or an enemy?

Cin. As a friend.

2. Pleb. That matter is answered directly.

4. Pleb. For your dwelling—briefly.

Cin. Briefly, I dwell by the Capitol.   25

3. Pleb. Your name, sir, truly.

Cin. Truly, my name is Cinna.

1. Pleb. Tear him to pieces! He's a conspirator.

Cin. I am Cinna the poet! I am Cinna the poet!

4. Pleb. Tear him for his bad verses! Tear him for his   30
bad verses!

Cin. I am not Cinna the conspirator.

4. Pleb. It is no matter; his name's Cinna! Pluck but
his name out of his heart, and turn him going.

3. Pleb. Tear him, tear him! Come, brands, ho! fire-   35
brands! To Brutus', to Cassius'! Burn all! Some to Decius'
house and some to Casca's; some to Ligarius'! Away, go!

Exeunt all the Plebeians.

THE TRAGEDY OF

JULIUS CÆSAR

ACT IV

IV. [i.] Antony, Octavius, and Lepidus plan the death of those who may be hostile to their cause. Lepidus goes to get Cæsar's will, and Octavius and Antony agree that they must speedily gather a military force to combat Brutus and Cassius.

11. **cut off some charge:** reduce our expense.
14. **slight:** of little value.

Trumpeters of the Roman army.
From Pierre duChoul, *Discours de la religion des anciens Romains* (1556).

ACT IV

[Scene I. The same. Antony's house.]

Enter *Antony, Octavius,* and *Lepidus.*

Ant. These many, then, shall die; their names are
pricked.
  Oct. Your brother too must die. Consent you, Lepidus?
  Lep. I do consent.
  Oct.   Prick him down, Antony.   5
  Lep. Upon condition Publius shall not live,
Who is your sister's son, Mark Antony.
  Ant. He shall not live. Look, with a spot I damn him.
But, Lepidus, go you to Cæsar's house.
Fetch the will hither, and we shall determine   10
How to cut off some charge in legacies.
  Lep. What? shall I find you here?
  Oct. Or here or at the Capitol.

                                        Exit Lepidus.

  Ant. This is a slight unmeritable man,
Meet to be sent on errands. Is it fit,   15
The threefold world divided, he should stand
One of the three to share it?
  Oct.   So you thought him,

64

38. **taste:** degree.
42. **staled:** cheapened; see I. [ii.] 78.
44. **property:** an object for our use.
46. **make head:** assemble our military forces.
50. **covert matters may be best disclosed:** the secret plans (of the enemy) may best be discovered.

And took his voice who should be pricked to die
In our black sentence and proscription.   20
   Ant. Octavius, I have seen more days than you;
And though we lay these honors on this man
To ease ourselves of divers sland'rous loads,
He shall but bear them as the ass bears gold,
To groan and sweat under the business,   25
Either led or driven as we point the way;
And having brought our treasure where we will,
Then take we down his load, and turn him off
(Like to the empty ass) to shake his ears
And graze in commons.   30
   Oct.   You may do your will;
But he's a tried and valiant soldier.
   Ant. So is my horse, Octavius, and for that
I do appoint him store of provender.
It is a creature that I teach to fight,   35
To wind, to stop, to run directly on,
His corporal motion governed by my spirit.
And, in some taste, is Lepidus but so.
He must be taught, and trained, and bid go forth:
A barren-spirited fellow; one that feeds   40
On objects, arts, and imitations
Which, out of use and staled by other men,
Begin his fashion. Do not talk of him,
But as a property. And now, Octavius,
Listen great things. Brutus and Cassius   45
Are levying powers. We must straight make head.
Therefore let our alliance be combined,
Our best friends made, and our best means stretched out;
And let us presently go sit in council
How covert matters may be best disclosed   50

52-3. **at the stake/ And bayed about with many enemies:** that is, in as perilous a position as a bear tied to a stage at the mercy of dogs. Such "bear baiting" was a popular sport in Elizabethan times.

⁙⁙⁙⁙⁙⁙⁙⁙⁙⁙⁙⁙⁙⁙⁙⁙⁙⁙⁙⁙⁙⁙⁙⁙⁙⁙⁙⁙⁙⁙

IV. [ii.] Brutus has become displeased with Cassius' actions and his friend Lucilius confirms that Cassius has seemed less friendly than formerly. Cassius comes to Brutus' tent to discuss their differences.

⁙⁙⁙⁙⁙⁙⁙⁙⁙⁙⁙⁙⁙⁙⁙⁙⁙⁙⁙⁙⁙⁙

6. **He greets me well:** that is, it's good news that Cassius has sent his greetings.

7. **In his own change, or by ill officers:** either as a result of a change in himself or because of the faulty carrying out of his commands by subordinates.

13. **regard:** proper respect (for your wishes).

17. **familiar instances:** indications of friendship.

And open perils surest answered.

  Oct. Let us do so; for we are at the stake
And bayed about with many enemies;
And some that smile have in their hearts, I fear,
Millions of mischiefs.   55

                     Exeunt.

[Scene II. The camp near Sardis. Before Brutus' tent.]

Drum. Enter *Brutus, Lucilius,* [*Lucius,*] and the *Army.*
      Titinius and *Pindarus* meet them.

  Bru. Stand ho!
  Lucil. Give the word, ho! and stand!
  Bru. What now, Lucilius? Is Cassius near?
  Lucil. He is at hand, and Pindarus is come
To do you salutation from his master.   5
  Bru. He greets me well. Your master, Pindarus,
In his own change, or by ill officers,
Hath given me some worthy cause to wish
Things done undone; but if he be at hand,
I shall be satisfied.   10
  Pin.   I do not doubt
But that my noble master will appear
Such as he is, full of regard and honor.
  Bru. He is not doubted. A word, Lucilius,
How he received you. Let me be resolved.   15
  Lucil. With courtesy and with respect enough,
But not with such familiar instances
Nor with such free and friendly conference

23. **enforced:** forced, unnatural.

25. **hollow:** faithless, insincere; **hot at hand:** fiery when checked.

26. **mettle:** spirit; see I. [ii.] 301.

28. **fall their crests:** droop their necks; **deceitful jades:** horses that do not live up to their high promise as winners.

29. **Sink in the trial:** fail when tested.

34. **gently:** slowly.

43. **sober form:** habitually grave behavior. Cassius means that Brutus' characteristic appearance of gravity and justice does not mean that he never is unjust.

45. **be content:** be calm, take it easy.

46. **griefs:** complaints.

As he hath used of old.

Bru.   Thou hast described   20
A hot friend cooling. Ever note, Lucilius,
When love begins to sicken and decay
It useth an enforced ceremony.
There are no tricks in plain and simple faith;
But hollow men, like horses hot at hand,   25
Make gallant show and promise of their mettle;
                         Low march within.
But when they should endure the bloody spur,
They fall their crests, and like deceitful jades
Sink in the trial. Comes his army on?

Lucil. They mean this night in Sardis to be quartered.   30
The greater part, the horse in general,
Are come with Cassius.

Bru.   Hark! He is arrived.
March gently on to meet him.

        Enter *Cassius* and his *Powers.*

Cass. Stand, ho!   35
Bru. Stand, ho! Speak the word along.
1. Sold. Stand!
2. Sold. Stand!
3. Sold. Stand!
Cass. Most noble brother, you have done me wrong.   40
Bru. Judge me, you gods! wrong I mine enemies?
And if not so, how should I wrong a brother?
Cass. Brutus, this sober form of yours hides wrongs,
And when you do them—
Bru.   Cassius, be content.   45
Speak your griefs softly. I do know you well.

50. **enlarge**: release, set forth.

▬▬▬▬▬▬▬▬▬▬▬▬▬▬▬▬▬▬▬

IV. [iii.] Brutus rebukes Cassius for condoning
an officer who took bribes and condemns Cassius'
own acquisitive tendencies. The two exchange bitter
words. After Cassius softens and they make peace,
Brutus tells Cassius that Portia is dead. Titinius
and Messala enter to confer on military strategy.
Brutus, overruling Cassius' objections, decides that
their forces should set off for Philippi to meet Antony and Octavius. Later, reading in his tent, Brutus
receives a visit from the Ghost of Cæsar, who de-
parts with the warning that Brutus will see him
again at Philippi.

▬▬▬▬▬▬▬▬▬▬▬▬▬▬▬

2. **noted**: marked with disgrace.
8. **nice**: trifling; **bear his comment**: be noticed.
10. **condemned to have**: judged as having.

Before the eyes of both our armies here
(Which should perceive nothing but love from us)
Let us not wrangle. Bid them move away.
Then in my tent, Cassius, enlarge your griefs,   50
And I will give you audience.
    Cass.   Pindarus,
Bid our commanders lead their charges off
A little from this ground.
    Bru. Lucilius, do you the like, and let no man   55
Come to our tent till we have done our conference.
Let Lucius and Titinius guard our door.

                                    Exeunt.

[Scene III. The same. Brutus' tent.]

Enter *Brutus* and *Cassius.*

    Cass. That you have wronged me doth appear in this:
You have condemned and noted Lucius Pella
For taking bribes here of the Sardians;
Wherein my letters, praying on his side,
Because I knew the man, were slighted off.   5
    Bru. You wronged yourself to write in such a case.
    Cass. In such a time as this it is not meet
That every nice offense should bear his comment.
    Bru. Let me tell you, Cassius, you yourself
Are much condemned to have an itching palm,   10
To sell and mart your offices for gold
To undeservers.
    Cass.   I an itching palm?

24. **But for supporting robbers:** Brutus introduces an argument for the occasion; his reasons for joining in the assassination of Cæsar were based on the likelihood of Cæsar's becoming a tyrant, not on his toleration of dishonesty.

28. **bay the moon:** proverbial: "The moon does not heed the barking of dogs"; to **bay the moon** therefore epitomizes futility.

30. **bait:** torment; see IV. [i.] 52-3.

32. **hedge me in:** attempt to control my conduct; another allusion to the bear surrounded by dogs may also be intended, in keeping with **bait** in line 30.

38. **Urge:** provoke.

43. **choler:** anger.

You know that you are Brutus that speaks this,
Or, by the gods, this speech were else your last!   15
    Bru. The name of Cassius honors this corruption,
And chastisement doth therefore hide his head.
    Cass. Chastisement?
    Bru. Remember March; the ides of March remember.
Did not great Julius bleed for justice' sake?   20
What villain touched his body that did stab
And not for justice? What, shall one of us,
That struck the foremost man of all this world
But for supporting robbers—shall we now
Contaminate our fingers with base bribes,   25
And sell the mighty space of our large honors
For so much trash as may be grasped thus?
I had rather be a dog and bay the moon
Than such a Roman.
    Cass.   Brutus, bait not me!   30
I'll not endure it. You forget yourself
To hedge me in. I am a soldier, I,
Older in practice, abler than yourself
To make conditions.
    Bru.   Go to! You are not, Cassius.   35
    Cass. I am.
    Bru. I say you are not.
    Cass. Urge me no more! I shall forget myself.
Have mind upon your health, tempt me no farther.
    Bru. Away, slight man!   40
    Cass. Is't possible?
    Bru.   Hear me, for I will speak.
Must I give way and room to your rash choler?
Shall I be frighted when a madman stares?
    Cass. O ye gods, ye gods! Must I endure all this?   45

50. **observe**: humor, pay respect to.
52. **digest**: contain within yourself.
58. **vaunting**: boasting.

Roman foot soldiers.

From Pierre duChoul, *Discours de la religion des anciens Romains*
(1556).

Bru. All this? Ay, more! Fret till your proud heart
   break.
Go show your slaves how choleric you are
And make your bondmen tremble. Must I budge?
Must I observe you? Must I stand and crouch   50
Under your testy humor? By the gods,
You shall digest the venom of your spleen,
Though it do split you; for from this day forth
I'll use you for my mirth, yea, for my laughter,
When you are waspish.   55
   Cass.   Is it come to this?
   Bru. You say you are a better soldier;
Let it appear so. Make your vaunting true,
And it shall please me well. For mine own part,
I shall be glad to learn of noble men.   60
   Cass. You wrong me every way! You wrong me, Brutus!
I said an elder soldier, not a better.
Did I say "better"?
   Bru.   If you did, I care not.
   Cass. When Cæsar lived he durst not thus have moved   65
   me.
   Bru. Peace, peace! You durst not so have tempted him.
   Cass. I durst not?
   Bru. No.
   Cass. What, durst not tempt him?   70
   Bru.   For your life you durst not.
   Cass. Do not presume too much upon my love.
I may do that I shall be sorry for.
   Bru. You have done that you should be sorry for.
There is no terror, Cassius, in your threats;   75
For I am armed so strong in honesty
That they pass by me as the idle wind,

84. **indirection**: dishonesty.

89. **rascal counters**: paltry tokens; **counters** were worthless or imitation coins and the word came to be used contemptuously for money itself.

107. **braved**: challenged.

108. **Checked**: reprimanded.

Which I respect not. I did send to you
For certain sums of gold, which you denied me,
For I can raise no money by vile means—   80
By heaven, I had rather coin my heart
And drop my blood for drachmas than to wring
From the hard hands of peasants their vile trash
By any indirection. I did send
To you for gold to pay my legions,   85
Which you denied me. Was that done like Cassius?
Should I have answered Caius Cassius so?
When Marcus Brutus grows so covetous
To lock such rascal counters from his friends,
Be ready, gods, with all your thunderbolts,   90
Dash him to pieces!
   Cass.   I denied you not.
   Bru. You did.
   Cass. I did not. He was but a fool that brought
My answer back. Brutus hath rived my heart.   95
A friend should bear his friend's infirmities,
But Brutus makes mine greater than they are.
   Bru. I do not, till you practice them on me.
   Cass. You love me not.
   Bru.   I do not like your faults.   100
   Cass. A friendly eye could never see such faults.
   Bru. A flatterer's would not, though they do appear
As huge as high Olympus.
   Cass. Come, Antony, and young Octavius, come!
Revenge yourselves alone on Cassius.   105
For Cassius is aweary of the world:
Hated by one he loves; braved by his brother;
Checked like a bondman; all his faults observed,

109. **learned and conned by rote**: learned by heart.

113. **Pluto's mine**: Pluto, classical god of the underworld, owned the riches in the earth since they occurred in his dominions.

121. **dishonor shall be humor**: the disrespect you show me shall be taken as due to your disposition.

Set in a notebook, learned and conned by rote
To cast into my teeth. O, I could weep   110
My spirit from mine eyes! There is my dagger,
And here my naked breast; within, a heart
Dearer than Pluto's mine, richer than gold:
If that thou be'st a Roman, take it forth.
I, that denied thee gold, will give my heart.   115
Strike as thou didst at Cæsar; for I know,
When thou didst hate him worst, thou lov'dst him better
Than ever thou lov'dst Cassius.
  Bru.   Sheathe your dagger.
Be angry when you will; it shall have scope.   120
Do what you will; dishonor shall be humor.
O Cassius, you are yoked with a lamb
That carries anger as the flint bears fire;
Who, much enforced, shows a hasty spark,
And straight is cold again.   125
  Cass.   Hath Cassius lived
To be but mirth and laughter to his Brutus
When grief and blood ill-tempered vexeth him?
  Bru. When I spoke that, I was ill-tempered too.
  Cass. Do you confess so much? Give me your hand.   130
  Bru. And my heart too.
  Cass.   O Brutus!
  Bru.   What's the matter?
  Cass. Have you not love enough to bear with me
When that rash humor which my mother gave me   135
Makes me forgetful?
  Bru.   Yes, Cassius, and from henceforth,
When you are over-earnest with your Brutus,
He'll think your mother chides, and leave you so.

153. **jigging**: rhyming.

154. **Companion**: fellow; a contemptuous expression.

164-65. **Of your philosophy you make no use/ If you give place to accidental evils**: that is, you do not live by the philosophy you profess if you are affected by the minor misfortunes of life.

Enter a *Poet* [followed by *Lucilius, Titinius,*
and *Lucius*].

Poet. Let me go in to see the generals!   140
There is some grudge between 'em. 'Tis not meet
They be alone.
  Lucil. You shall not come to them.
  Poet. Nothing but death shall stay me.
  Cass. How now? What's the matter?   145
  Poet. For shame, you generals! What do you mean?
Love and be friends, as two such men should be,
For I have seen more years, I'm sure, than ye.
  Cass. Ha, ha! How vilely doth this cynic rhyme!
  Bru. Get you hence, sirrah! Saucy fellow, hence!   150
  Cass. Bear with him, Brutus. 'Tis his fashion.
  Bru. I'll know his humor when he knows his time.
What should the wars do with these jigging fools?
Companion, hence!
  Cass.   Away, away, be gone!   155
                                         Exit Poet.
  Bru. Lucilius and Titinius, bid the commanders
Prepare to lodge their companies tonight.
  Cass. And come yourselves, and bring Messala with
    you
Immediately to us.   160
              [*Exeunt Lucilius and Titinius.*]
  Bru.   Lucius, a bowl of wine.
                              [*Exit Lucius.*]
  Cass. I did not think you could have been so angry.
  Bru. O Cassius, I am sick of many griefs.
  Cass. Of your philosophy you make no use
If you give place to accidental evils.   165

171. **Upon:** by reason of; see III. [i.] 236.
178. **Even:** exactly.
187. **call in question:** discuss.

Roman soldiers.

From Pierre duChoul, *Discours de la religion des anciens Romains*
(1556).

Bru. No man bears sorrow better. Portia is dead.

Cass. Ha! Portia?

Bru. She is dead.

Cass. How scaped I killing when I crossed you so?
O insupportable and touching loss!   170
Upon what sickness?

Bru.   Impatient of my absence,
And grief that young Octavius with Mark Antony
Have made themselves so strong—for with her death
That tidings came—with this she fell distract,   175
And (her attendants absent) swallowed fire.

Cass. And died so?

Bru.   Even so.

Cass.   O ye immortal gods!

Enter Boy, [*Lucius*,] with wine and tapers.

Bru. Speak no more of her. Give me a bowl of wine. 180
In this I bury all unkindness, Cassius.   *Drinks.*

Cass. My heart is thirsty for that noble pledge.
Fill, Lucius, till the wine o'erswell the cup.
I cannot drink too much of Brutus' love.

                              [*Drinks. Exit Lucius.*]

Enter *Titinius* and *Messala*.

Bru. Come in, Titinius! Welcome, good Messala.   185
Now sit we close about this taper here
And call in question our necessities.

Cass. Portia, art thou gone?

Bru.   No more, I pray you.
Messala, I have here received letters   190

194. **tenure:** tenor, import.

219. **I have as much of this in art as you:** that is,
I know as much about the theory of stoicism as you
do.

222. **presently:** at once.

ICONES.

ZENO CITTICVS.

Zeno, founder of the Stoic philosophy.
From Jean de Tournes, *Insignium aliquot virorum icones* (1559).

That young Octavius and Mark Antony
Come down upon us with a mighty power,
Bending their expedition toward Philippi.
    Mes. Myself have letters of the selfsame tenure.
    Bru. With what addition?   195
    Mes. That by proscription and bills of outlawry
Octavius, Antony, and Lepidus
Have put to death an hundred senators.
    Bru. Therein our letters do not well agree.
Mine speak of seventy senators that died   200
By their proscriptions, Cicero being one.
    Cass. Cicero one?
    Mes.   Cicero is dead,
And by that order of proscription.
Had you your letters from your wife, my lord?   205
    Bru. No, Messala.
    Mes. Nor nothing in your letters writ of her?
    Bru. Nothing, Messala.
    Mes.   That methinks is strange.
    Bru. Why ask you? Hear you aught of her in yours? 210
    Mes. No, my lord.
    Bru. Now as you are a Roman, tell me true.
    Mes. Then like a Roman bear the truth I tell,
For certain she is dead, and by strange manner.
    Bru. Why, farewell, Portia. We must die, Messala.   215
With meditating that she must die once,
I have the patience to endure it now.
    Mes. Even so great men great losses should endure.
    Cass. I have as much of this in art as you,
But yet my nature could not bear it so.   220
    Bru. Well, to our work alive. What do you think
Of marching to Philippi presently?

232. **Do stand but in a forced affection:** are not genuinely friendly to our side.

241. **Under your pardon:** that is, by your leave, I will continue.

248. **Omitted:** neglected.

249. **bound in:** confined to.

253. **with your will:** as you wish.

Cass. I do not think it good.

Bru.   Your reason?

Cass.   This it is: 225
'Tis better that the enemy seek us.
So shall he waste his means, weary his soldiers,
Doing himself offense, whilst we, lying still,
Are full of rest, defense, and nimbleness.

    Bru. Good reasons must of force give place to better. 230
The people 'twixt Philippi and this ground
Do stand but in a forced affection,
For they have grudged us contribution.
The enemy, marching along by them,
By them shall make a fuller number up,   235
Come on refreshed, new-added, and encouraged;
From which advantage shall we cut him off
If at Philippi we do face him there,
These people at our back.

    Cass.   Hear me, good brother.   240

    Bru. Under your pardon. You must note beside
That we have tried the utmost of our friends,
Our legions are brimful, our cause is ripe.
The enemy increaseth every day;
We, at the height, are ready to decline.   245
There is a tide in the affairs of men
Which, taken at the flood, leads on to fortune;
Omitted, all the voyage of their life
Is bound in shallows and in miseries.
On such a full sea are we now afloat,   250
And we must take the current when it serves
Or lose our ventures.

    Cass.   Then, with your will, go on.

257. **niggard**: treat in a niggardly fashion, slight.
260. **hence**: go or move hence; the verb is understood.
277. **o'erwatched**: worn out from lack of sleep.

We'll along ourselves and meet them at Philippi.

   Bru. The deep of night is crept upon our talk   255
And nature must obey necessity,
Which we will niggard with a little rest.
There is no more to say?

   Cass.   No more. Good night.
Early tomorrow will we rise and hence.   260

   Bru. Lucius! (*Enter Lucius.*) My gown.

                         [*Exit Lucius.*]

     Farewell, good Messala.
Good night, Titinius. Noble, noble Cassius,
Good night and good repose!

   Cass.   O my dear brother,   265
This was an ill beginning of the night!
Never come such division 'tween our souls!
Let it not, Brutus.

            Enter *Lucius*, with the gown.

   Bru.   Everything is well.

   Cass. Good night, my lord.   270

   Bru.   Good night, good brother.

   Tit., Mes. Good night, Lord Brutus.

   Bru.   Farewell every one.

       Exeunt [*Cassius, Titinius, and Messala*].
Give me the gown. Where is thy instrument?

   Luc. Here in the tent.   275

   Bru.   What, thou speak'st drowsily?
Poor knave, I blame thee not, thou art o'erwatched.
Call Claudius and some other of my men;
I'll have them sleep on cushions in my tent.

   Luc. Varro and Claudius!   280

285-86. **watch your pleasure:** remain wakeful as long as it pleases you.

295. **an't:** if it.

306. **mace:** both a weapon and an instrument of office; **slumber** is pictured as taking Lucius in charge, as though it were a human official.

Enter Varro *and* Claudius.

Var. Calls my lord?
Bru. I pray you, sirs, lie in my tent and sleep.
It may be I shall raise you by-and-by
On business to my brother Cassius.
   Var. So please you, we will stand and watch your 285
     pleasure.
   Bru. I will not have it so. Lie down, good sirs.
It may be I shall otherwise bethink me.
                    [Varro and Claudius lie down.]
Look, Lucius, here's the book I sought for so;
I put it in the pocket of my gown.   290
   Luc. I was sure your lordship did not give it me.
   Bru. Bear with me, good boy, I am much forgetful.
Canst thou hold up thy heavy eyes awhile,
And touch thy instrument a strain or two?
   Luc. Ay, my lord, an't please you.   295
   Bru.   It does, my boy.
I trouble thee too much, but thou art willing.
   Luc. It is my duty, sir.
   Bru. I should not urge thy duty past thy might.
I know young bloods look for a time of rest.   300
   Luc. I have slept, my lord, already.
   Bru. It was well done; and thou shalt sleep again;
I will not hold thee long. If I do live,
I will be good to thee.
           Music, and a song. [Lucius falls asleep.]
This is a sleepy tune. O murd'rous slumber!   305
Layest thou thy leaden mace upon my boy,
That plays thee music? Gentle knave, good night.
I will not do thee so much wrong to wake thee.

A Roman legionary.

From Pierre duChoul, *Discours de la religion des anciens Romains*
(1556).

If thou dost nod, thou break'st thy instrument;
I'll take it from thee; and, good boy, good night.   310
Let me see, let me see. Is not the leaf turned down
Where I left reading? Here it is, I think.   [*Sits.*]

Enter the *Ghost of Cæsar*.

How ill this taper burns! Ha! Who comes here?
I think it is the weakness of mine eyes
That shapes this monstrous apparition.   315
It comes upon me. Art thou anything?
Art thou some god, some angel, or some devil,
That mak'st my blood cold and my hair to stare?
Speak to me what thou art.
  Ghost. Thy evil spirit, Brutus.   320
  Bru.   Why com'st thou?
  Ghost. To tell thee thou shalt see me at Philippi.
  Bru. Well; then I shall see thee again?
  Ghost. Ay, at Philippi.
  Bru. Why, I will see thee at Philippi then.   325
                       [*Exit Ghost.*]
Now I have taken heart thou vanishest.
Ill spirit, I would hold more talk with thee.
Boy! Lucius! Varro! Claudius! Sirs! Awake!
Claudius!
  Luc. The strings, my lord, are false.   330
  Bru. He thinks he still is at his instrument.
Lucius, awake!
  Luc. My lord?
  Bru. Didst thou dream, Lucius, that thou so criedst
     out?   335
  Luc. My lord, I do not know that I did cry.

349. **betimes**: promptly; see II. [i.] 123.

Bru. Yes, that thou didst. Didst thou see anything?
Luc. Nothing, my lord.
Bru. Sleep again, Lucius. Sirrah Claudius!
[*To Varro*] Fellow thou, awake!   340
Var. My lord?
Clau. My lord?
Bru. Why did you so cry out, sirs, in your sleep?
Both. Did we, my lord?
Bru.   Ay. Saw you anything?   345
Var. No, my lord, I saw nothing.
Clau.   Nor I, my lord.
Bru. Go and commend me to my brother Cassius.
Bid him set on his pow'rs betimes before,
And we will follow.   350
Both.   It shall be done, my lord.
                                        Exeunt.

THE TRAGEDY OF
JULIUS CÆSAR

ACT V

V. [i.] The forces of Antony and Brutus meet, and Brutus, Cassius, Antony, and Octavius exchange taunts before engaging.

▬▬▬▬▬▬▬▬▬▬▬▬▬▬

4. **battles:** battle forces, hosts.

5. **warn us:** call us to battle.

7. **bosoms:** confidence.

8. **could be content:** would be satisfied.

10. **With fearful bravery:** handsomely arrayed in a show of defiance which hides their real fear.

15. **bloody sign of battle:** North's translation of Plutarch relates that the signal of battle hung out in the camp of Brutus and Cassius was a scarlet coat.

ACT V

[Scene I. The plains of Philippi.]

Enter Octavius, Antony, and their Army.

Oct. Now, Antony, our hopes are answered.
You said the enemy would not come down
But keep the hills and upper regions.
It proves not so, their battles are at hand.
They mean to warn us at Philippi here,   5
Answering before we do demand of them.
   Ant. Tut! I am in their bosoms and I know
Wherefore they do it. They could be content
To visit other places, and come down
With fearful bravery, thinking by this face   10
To fasten in our thoughts that they have courage.
But 'tis not so.

Enter a Messenger.

   Mess.   Prepare you, generals,
The enemy comes on in gallant show;
Their bloody sign of battle is hung out,   15

17. **softly**: slowly.

20. **exigent**: exigency, crisis.

36. **Hybla bees**: Mount Hybla in Sicily was famous for its honey. Shakespeare often uses a place name as an adjective; see I. i. 61.

A parley on the battlefield.

From Andrea Alciati, *Emblematum* (1534).

And something to be done immediately.

   Ant. Octavius, lead your battle softly on
Upon the left hand of the even field.

   Oct. Upon the right hand I. Keep thou the left.

   Ant. Why do you cross me in this exigent?   20

   Oct. I do not cross you; but I will do so.

                           March.

Drum. Enter Brutus, Cassius, *and their* Army; [*Lucilius,*
       Titinius, Messala, *and others*].

   Bru. They stand and would have parley.

   Cass. Stand fast, Titinius. We must out and talk.

   Oct. Mark Antony, shall we give sign of battle?

   Ant. No, Cæsar, we will answer on their charge.   25
Make forth. The generals would have some words.

   Oct. Stir not until the signal.

   Bru. Words before blows. Is it so, countrymen?

   Oct. Not that we love words better, as you do.

   Bru. Good words are better than bad strokes, Octavius.   30

   Ant. In your bad strokes, Brutus, you give good words;
Witness the hole you made in Cæsar's heart,
Crying "Long live! Hail, Cæsar!"

   Cass.   Antony,
The posture of your blows are yet unknown;   35
But for your words, they rob the Hybla bees,
And leave them honeyless.

   Ant.   Not stingless too.

   Bru. O yes, and soundless too!
For you have stol'n their buzzing, Antony,   40
And very wisely threat before you sting.

   Ant. Villains! you did not so when your vile daggers

52. **proof:** trial; that is, the settlement of the argument by battle.

57. **another Cæsar:** i.e., himself.

58. **Have added slaughter:** become another victim.

65. **peevish:** silly, trifling.

66. **a masker and a reveller:** Antony's fondness for self-amusement and debauchery was well known; a masker is one who indulges in masques, which were entertainments combining music, dance, and masquerade.

67. **Old Cassius still:** that is, Cassius' tongue is as sharp as ever.

71. **stomachs:** taste for battle, i.e., courage.

Hacked one another in the sides of Cæsar.
You showed your teeth like apes, and fawned like hounds,
And bowed like bondmen, kissing Cæsar's feet;   45
Whilst damned Casca, like a cur, behind
Struck Cæsar on the neck. O you flatterers!

Cass. Flatterers? Now, Brutus, thank yourself!
This tongue had not offended so today
If Cassius might have ruled.   50

Oct. Come, come, the cause! If arguing make us sweat,
The proof of it will turn to redder drops.
Look,
I draw a sword against conspirators.
When think you that the sword goes up again?   55
Never, till Cæsar's three-and-thirty wounds
Be well avenged, or till another Cæsar
Have added slaughter to the sword of traitors.

Bru. Cæsar, thou canst not die by traitors' hands
Unless thou bring'st them with thee.   60

Oct.   So I hope.
I was not born to die on Brutus' sword.

Bru. O, if thou wert the noblest of thy strain,
Young man, thou couldst not die more honorable.

Cass. A peevish schoolboy, worthless of such honor,   65
Joined with a masker and a reveller!

Ant. Old Cassius still.

Oct.   Come, Antony. Away!
Defiance, traitors, hurl we in your teeth.
If you dare fight today, come to the field;   70
If not, when you have stomachs.

                    Exeunt Octavius, Antony, and Army.

Cass. Why, now blow wind, swell billow, and swim
    bark!

80. **as this very day:** as has no effect on the meaning of this phrase. Shakespeare more than once uses as redundantly in similar circumstances.

83. **set:** stake.

85. **held Epicurus strong:** had a firm belief in the theories of Epicurus, referring specifically to his denial of supernatural interference in human affairs and consequent disbelief in omens.

87. **presage:** foretell as omens.

88. **former:** foremost.

91. **consorted:** accompanied.

95. **As we:** as if we.

101. **constantly:** firmly.

EPICVRVS ATHENIENSIS.

The philosopher Epicurus.

From Jean de Tournes, *Insignium aliquot virorum icones* (1559).

The storm is up, and all is on the hazard.

Bru. Ho, Lucilius! Hark, a word with you.   75

                    Lucilius and Messala stand forth.

Lucil.   My lord?

                    [*Brutus and Lucilius converse apart.*]

Cass. Messala.

Mes.   What says my general?

Cass.   Messala,

This is my birthday; as this very day   80

Was Cassius born. Give me thy hand, Messala.

Be thou my witness that against my will

(As Pompey was) am I compelled to set

Upon one battle all our liberties.

You know that I held Epicurus strong   85

And his opinion. Now I change my mind

And partly credit things that do presage.

Coming from Sardis, on our former ensign

Two mighty eagles fell, and there they perched,

Gorging and feeding from our soldiers' hands,   90

Who to Philippi here consorted us.

This morning are they fled away and gone,

And in their steads do ravens, crows, and kites

Fly o'er our heads and downward look on us

As we were sickly prey. Their shadows seem   95

A canopy most fatal, under which

Our army lies, ready to give up the ghost.

Mes. Believe not so.

Cass.   I but believe it partly,

For I am fresh of spirit and resolved   100

To meet all perils very constantly.

Bru. Even so, Lucilius.

Cass.   Now, most noble Brutus,

104. **stand friendly:** this is not a statement of fact but a hope.

106. **rest:** remain; **still:** always; see III. [i.] 158.

115-16. **prevent/ The time of life:** forestall the natural end of life.

117. **stay:** wait for.

Standard-bearers of the Roman army.
From Pierre duChoul, *Discours de la religion des anciens Romains* (1556).

The gods today stand friendly, that we may,
Lovers in peace, lead on our days to age!   105
But since the affairs of men rest still incertain,
Let's reason with the worst that may befall.
If we do lose this battle, then is this
The very last time we shall speak together.
What are you then determined to do?   110
  Bru. Even by the rule of that philosophy
By which I did blame Cato for the death
Which he did give himself—I know not how,
But I do find it cowardly and vile,
For fear of what might fall, so to prevent   115
The time of life—arming myself with patience
To stay the providence of some high powers
That govern us below.
  Cass.   Then, if we lose this battle,
You are contented to be led in triumph   120
Thorough the streets of Rome.
  Bru. No, Cassius, no. Think not, thou noble Roman,
That ever Brutus will go bound to Rome.
He bears too great a mind. But this same day
Must end that work the ides of March begun,   125
And whether we shall meet again I know not.
Therefore our everlasting farewell take.
For ever and for ever farewell, Cassius!
If we do meet again, why, we shall smile;
If not, why then this parting was well made.   130
  Cass. For ever and for ever farewell, Brutus!
If we do meet again, we'll smile indeed;
If not, 'tis true this parting was well made.
  Bru. Why then, lead on. O that a man might know
The end of this day's business ere it come!   135

V. [ii.] Brutus dispatches Messala with instructions for his legions.

●●●●●●●●●●●●●●●●●●●●●●●●●●

Entrance. **Alarum:** a trumpet call to arms.
1. **bills:** notes.
4. **cold demeanor:** sluggish action.

●●●●●●●●●●●●●●●●●●●●●●●●●●●●●●●●

V. [iii.] Cassius, mistakenly thinking that Titinius has been captured, forces his slave Pindarus to kill him with the very sword with which he killed Cæsar. When Titinius finds Cassius, he places a wreath of victory on his brow and kills himself.

●●●●●●●●●●●●●●●●●●●●

3. **ensign:** both the standard and the man who bore it.

But it sufficeth that the day will end,
And then the end is known. Come, ho! Away!

                                    Exeunt.

[Scene II. The same. The field of battle.]

Alarum. Enter *Brutus* and *Messala.*

Bru. Ride, ride, Messala, ride, and give these bills
Unto the legions on the other side.

                                Loud alarum.

Let them set on at once; for I perceive
But cold demeanor in Octavius' wing,
And sudden push gives them the overthrow.   5
Ride, ride, Messala! Let them all come down.

                                    Exeunt.

[Scene III. Another part of the field.]

Alarums. Enter *Cassius* and *Titinius.*

Cass. O, look, Titinius, look! The villains fly!
Myself have to mine own turned enemy.
This ensign here of mine was turning back;
I slew the coward and did take it from him.
Tit. O Cassius, Brutus gave the word too early,   5

26. **his**: its; **compass**: full circuit.

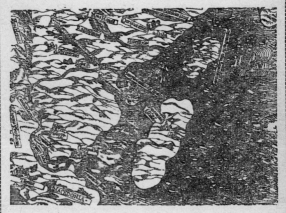

A sixteenth-century map of the region of Philippi.
From Pierre Belon, *Les observations de plusieurs singularitez*
(1588).

Who, having some advantage on Octavius,
Took it too eagerly. His soldiers fell to spoil,
Whilst we by Antony are all enclosed.

Enter *Pindarus.*

Pin. Fly further off, my lord! fly further off!
Mark Antony is in your tents, my lord.   10
Fly, therefore, noble Cassius, fly far off!
  Cass. This hill is far enough. Look, look, Titinius!
Are those my tents where I perceive the fire?
  Tit. They are, my lord.
  Cass.   Titinius, if thou lovest me,   15
Mount thou my horse and hide thy spurs in him
Till he have brought thee up to yonder troops
And here again, that I may rest assured
Whether yond troops are friend or enemy.
  Tit. I will be here again even with a thought.   *Exit.*   20
  Cass. Go, Pindarus, get higher on that hill.
My sight was ever thick. Regard Titinius,
And tell me what thou not'st about the field.
                    [*Pindarus ascends the hill.*]
This day I breathed first. Time is come round,
And where I did begin, there shall I end.   25
My life is run his compass. Sirrah, what news?
  Pin. (*Above*) O my lord!
  Cass. What news?
  Pin. [*Above*] Titinius is enclosed round about
With horsemen that make to him on the spur.   30
Yet he spurs on. Now they are almost on him.
Now, Titinius!

46. **hilts:** this plural form is common in Elizabethan times.

55. **change:** exchange.

Now some light. O, he lights too! He's ta'en. (*Shout.*)
    And hark!
They shout for joy.   35
    Cass.   Come down; behold no more.
O coward that I am to live so long
To see my best friend ta'en before my face!

                Enter *Pindarus* [from above].

Come hither, sirrah.
In Parthia did I take thee prisoner,   40
And then I swore thee, saving of thy life,
That whatsoever I did bid thee do,
Thou shouldst attempt it. Come now, keep thine oath.
Now be a freeman, and with this good sword,
That ran through Cæsar's bowels, search this bosom.   45
Stand not to answer. Here, take thou the hilts,
And when my face is covered, as 'tis now,
Guide thou the sword. [*Pindarus stabs him.*]—Cæsar,
    thou art revenged
Even with the sword that killed thee.   [*Dies.*] 50
    Pin. So, I am free, yet would not so have been,
Durst I have done my will. O Cassius!
Far from this country Pindarus shall run,
Where never Roman shall take note of him.   [*Exit.*]

                Enter *Titinius* and *Messala*.

    Mes. It is but change, Titinius; for Octavius   55
Is overthrown by noble Brutus' power,
As Cassius' legions are by Antony.
    Tit. These tidings will well comfort Cassius.

72. **Mistrust of good success:** i.e., doubt of succeeding.

87. **brave:** noble.

Mes. Where did you leave him?
Tit.   All disconsolate,   60
With Pindarus his bondman, on this hill.
  Mes. Is not that he that lies upon the ground?
  Tit. He lies not like the living. O my heart!
  Mes. Is not that he?
  Tit.   No, this was he, Messala,   65
But Cassius is no more. O setting sun,
As in thy red rays thou dost sink to night,
So in his red blood Cassius' day is set!
The sun of Rome is set. Our day is gone;
Clouds, dews, and dangers come; our deeds are done!   70
Mistrust of my success hath done this deed.
  Mes. Mistrust of good success hath done this deed.
O hateful Error, Melancholy's child,
Why dost thou show to the apt thoughts of men
The things that are not? O Error, soon conceived,   75
Thou never com'st unto a happy birth,
But kill'st the mother that engend'red thee!
  Tit. What, Pindarus! Where art thou, Pindarus?
  Mes. Seek him, Titinius, whilst I go to meet
The noble Brutus, thrusting this report   80
Into his ears. I may say "thrusting" it;
For piercing steel and darts envenomed
Shall be as welcome to the ears of Brutus
As tidings of this sight.
  Tit.   Hie you, Messala,   85
And I will seek for Pindarus the while.

                            [*Exit Messala.*]
Why didst thou send me forth, brave Cassius?
Did I not meet thy friends, and did not they
Put on my brows this wreath of victory

104. **proper**: personal; the use of **proper** with **own** merely makes it more emphatic.

106. **whe'r**: whether; see I. i. 64.

110. **fellow**: match; **mo**: more; see II. [i.] 73.

A Roman wreath of victory.

From Claude Guichard, *Funerailles, & diverses manieres* (1581).

And bid me give it thee? Didst thou not hear their shouts?   90
Alas, thou hast misconstrued everything!
But hold thee, take this garland on thy brow.
Thy Brutus bid me give it thee, and I
Will do his bidding. Brutus, come apace
And see how I regarded Caius Cassius.   95
By your leave, gods. This is a Roman's part.
Come, Cassius' sword, and find Titinius' heart.   *Dies.*

Alarum. Enter *Brutus, Messala, Young Cato, Strato,
        Volumnius,* and *Lucilius.*

Bru. Where, where, Messala, doth his body lie?
Mes. Lo, yonder, and Titinius mourning it.
Bru. Titinius' face is upward.   100
Cato.   He is slain.
Bru. O Julius Cæsar, thou art mighty yet!
Thy spirit walks abroad and turns our swords
In our own proper entrails.   *Low alarums.*
Cato.   Brave Titinius!   105
Look whe'r he have not crowned dead Cassius.
Bru. Are yet two Romans living such as these?
The last of all the Romans, fare thee well!
It is impossible that ever Rome
Should breed thy fellow. Friends, I owe mo tears   110
To this dead man than you shall see me pay.
I shall find time, Cassius; I shall find time.
Come therefore, and to Thasos send his body.
His funerals shall not be in our camp,
Lest it discomfort us. Lucilius, come;   115
And come, young Cato. Let us to the field.
Labeo and Flavius set our battles on.

V. [iv.] The fortunes of war begin to go against Brutus' side. Lucilius is captured and he assures Antony that Brutus himself will never be taken alive.

10. **bravely:** nobly; see V. [iii.] 87.

MARCVS PORTIVS CATO QVÆSTOR
SECVNDVM CONSVL TRIBV-
NVS MILITVM.

Marcus Cato.

From Jean de Tournes, *Insignium aliquot virorum icones* (1559).

'Tis three o'clock; and, Romans, yet ere night
We shall try fortune in a second fight.

Exeunt.

[Scene IV. Another part of the field.]

Alarum. Enter *Brutus, Messala,* [*Young*] *Cato, Lucilius,*
and *Flavius.*

Bru. Yet, countrymen, O, yet hold up your heads!
Cato. What bastard doth not? Who will go with me?
I will proclaim my name about the field.
I am the son of Marcus Cato, ho!
A foe to tyrants, and my country's friend.   5
I am the son of Marcus Cato, ho!

Enter *Soldiers* and fight.

Bru. And I am Brutus, Marcus Brutus I!
Brutus, my country's friend! Know me for Brutus! [*Exit.*]
                                [*Young Cato falls.*]
Lucil. O young and noble Cato, art thou down?
Why, now thou diest as bravely as Titinius,   10
And mayst be honored, being Cato's son.
1. Sold. Yield, or thou diest.
Lucil.   Only I yield to die.
[*Offering money*] There is so much that thou wilt kill me
   straight.   15
Kill Brutus, and be honored in his death.
1. Sold. We must not. A noble prisoner!

V. [v.] Facing defeat, Brutus kills himself. The victorious Antony and Octavius promise all honorable rites of burial for their noble adversary.

Archers.

From Pierre duChoul, *Discours de la religion des anciens Romains* (1556).

Enter *Antony*.

2. Sold. Room ho! Tell Antony Brutus is ta'en.

1. Sold. I'll tell the news. Here comes the general.

Brutus is ta'en! Brutus is ta'en, my lord!   20

Ant. Where is he?

Lucil. Safe, Antony; Brutus is safe enough.

I dare assure thee that no enemy

Shall ever take alive the noble Brutus.

The gods defend him from so great a shame!   25

When you do find him, or alive or dead,

He will be found like Brutus, like himself.

Ant. This is not Brutus, friend; but, I assure you,

A prize no less in worth. Keep this man safe;

Give him all kindness. I had rather have   30

Such men my friends than enemies. Go on,

And see whe'r Brutus be alive or dead;

And bring us word unto Octavius' tent

How every thing is chanced.

Exeunt.

[Scene V. Another part of the field.]

Enter *Brutus, Dardanius, Clitus, Strato,* and *Volumnius*.

Bru. Come, poor remains of friends, rest on this rock.

Cli. Statilius showed the torchlight, but, my lord,

He came not back. He is or ta'en or slain.

Bru. Sit thee down, Clitus. Slaying is the word.

It is a deed in fashion. Hark thee, Clitus.   [*Whispers.*]   5

21. several: separate.
27. pit: grave.

A legionary of the later Roman Empire.

From Pierre duChoul, *Discours de la religion des anciens Romains* (1556).

Cli. What, I, my lord? No, not for all the world!

Bru. Peace then. No words.

Cli.   I'll rather kill myself.

Bru. Hark thee, Dardanius.   [*Whispers.*]

Dar.   Shall I do such a deed?   10

Cli. O Dardanius!

Dar. O Clitus!

Cli. What ill request did Brutus make to thee?

Dar. To kill him, Clitus. Look, he meditates.

Cli. Now is that noble vessel full of grief,   15
That it runs over even at his eyes.

Bru. Come hither, good Volumnius. List a word.

Vol. What says my lord?

Bru.   Why this, Volumnius.
The ghost of Cæsar hath appeared to me   20
Two several times by night—at Sardis once,
And this last night here in Philippi fields.
I know my hour is come.

Vol.   Not so, my lord.

Bru. Nay, I am sure it is, Volumnius.   25
Thou seest the world, Volumnius, how it goes.
Our enemies have beat us to the pit.

                                    Low alarums.

It is more worthy to leap in ourselves
Than tarry till they push us. Good Volumnius,
Thou know'st that we two went to school together.   30
Even for that our love of old, I prithee
Hold thou my sword-hilts whilst I run on it.

Vol. That's not an office for a friend, my lord.

                                    Alarum still.

Cli. Fly, fly, my lord! There is no tarrying here.

Bru. Farewell to you; and you; and you, Volumnius.   35

51. **of a good respect**: that is, well thought of; see I. [ii.] 64.

52. **smatch**: smack, taste.

The death of Brutus.

From Jean Baudoin, *Recueil d'emblemes divers* (1638-1639).

Strato, thou hast been all this while asleep.
Farewell to thee too, Strato. Countrymen,
My heart doth joy that yet in all my life
I found no man but he was true to me.
I shall have glory by this losing day   40
More than Octavius and Mark Antony
By this vile conquest shall attain unto.
So fare you well at once, for Brutus' tongue
Hath almost ended his life's history.
Night hangs upon mine eyes; my bones would rest,   45
That have but labored to attain this hour.
                    Alarum. Cry within: Fly, fly, fly!
    Cli. Fly, my lord, fly!
    Bru.   Hence! I will follow.
            [*Exeunt Clitus, Dardanius, and Volumnius.*]
I prithee, Strato, stay thou by thy lord.   50
Thou art a fellow of a good respect;
Thy life hath had some smatch of honor in it.
Hold then my sword, and turn away thy face
While I do run upon it. Wilt thou, Strato?
    Stra. Give me your hand first. Fare you well, my lord.   55
    Bru. Farewell, good Strato. Cæsar, now be still.
I killed not thee with half so good a will.   *Dies.*

Alarum. Retreat. Enter *Octavius, Antony, Messala, Lu-
            cilius,* and the *Army.*

    Oct. What man is that?
    Mes. My master's man. Strato, where is thy master?
    Stra. Free from the bondage you are in, Messala.   60
The conquerors can but make a fire of him;
For Brutus only overcame himself,

66. **entertain:** hire.

68. **prefer:** recommend.

77-8. **in a general honest thought/ And common good to all:** with honorable concern for the good of the whole commonwealth.

85. **ordered:** handled, treated.

87. **part:** share.

And no man else hath honor by his death.
   Lucil. So Brutus should be found. I thank thee, Brutus,
That thou hast proved Lucilius' saying true.   65
   Oct. All that served Brutus, I will entertain them.
Fellow, wilt thou bestow thy time with me?
   Stra. Ay, if Messala will prefer me to you.
   Oct. Do so, good Messala.
   Mes. How died my master, Strato?   70
   Stra. I held the sword, and he did run on it.
   Mes. Octavius, then take him to follow thee,
That did the latest service to my master.
   Ant. This was the noblest Roman of them all.
All the conspirators save only he   75
Did that they did in envy of great Cæsar;
He, only in a general honest thought
And common good to all, made one of them.
His life was gentle, and the elements
So mixed in him that Nature might stand up   80
And say to all the world, "This was a man!"
   Oct. According to his virtue let us use him,
With all respect and rites of burial.
Within my tent his bones tonight shall lie,
Most like a soldier, ordered honorably.   85
So call the field to rest, and let's away
To part the glories of this happy day.
                           Exeunt omnes.

Famous Lines and Phrases

Beware the ides of March.   [Soothsayer—I. ii. 21]

. . . he doth bestride the narrow world
Like a Colossus, and we petty men
Walk under his huge legs and peep about
To find ourselves dishonorable graves.   [Cassius—I. ii. 141-44]

The fault, dear Brutus, is not in our stars,
But in ourselves . . .   [Cassius—I. ii. 146-47]

Upon what meat doth this our Cæsar feed
That he is grown so great?   [Cassius—I. ii. 155-56]

Let me have men about me that are fat . . .
                                             [Cæsar—I. ii. 199]

. . . but for mine own part, it was Greek to me.
                                             [Casca—I. ii. 288-89]

Cowards die many times before their deaths;
The valiant never taste of death but once.   [Cæsar—II. ii. 33-4]

Danger knows full well
That Cæsar is more dangerous than he.
We are two lions littered in one day,
And I the elder and more terrible . . .   [Cæsar—II. ii. 46-9]

Know, Cæsar doth not wrong, nor without cause
Will he be satisfied.   [Cæsar—III. i. 51-2]

Et tu, Brute?—Then fall Cæsar!   [Cæsar—III. i. 84]

Key to Famous Lines and Phrases

O mighty Cæsar! dost thou lie so low?
Are all thy conquests, glories, triumphs, spoils,
Shrunk to this little measure?   [Antony—III. i. 161-63]

Thou art the ruins of the noblest man
That ever lived in the tide of times.   [Antony—III. i. 277-78]

Cry "Havoc!" and let slip the dogs of war . . .
                                        [Antony—III. i. 294]

Romans, countrymen, and lovers, hear me for my cause . . .
                                        [Brutus—III. ii. 14]

Friends, Romans, countrymen, lend me your ears;
I come to bury Cæsar, not to praise him.
The evil that men do lives after them;
The good is oft interred with their bones.
                                        [Antony—III. ii. 80-83]

Ambition should be made of sterner stuff.
                                        [Antony—III. ii. 99]

O judgment, thou art fled to brutish beasts,
And men have lost their reason!   [Antony—III. ii. 111-12]

This was the most unkindest cut of all . . .
                                        [Antony—III. ii. 194]

There is a tide in the affairs of men
Which, taken at the flood, leads on to fortune . . .
                                        [Brutus—IV. iii. 246-47]

O Julius Cæsar, thou art mighty yet!
Thy spirit walks abroad and turns our swords
In our own proper entrails.   [Brutus—V. iii. 102-4]

This was the noblest Roman of them all. . . .
His life was gentle, and the elements
So mixed in him that Nature might stand up
And say to all the world, "This was a man!"
                                        [Antony—V. v. 74-81]

The FOLGER LIBRARY General Reader's.

SHAKESPEARE

Distinguished editions of the plays and poems edited by Louis B. Wright and Virginia A. LaMar.

The text is printed on right hand pages only, with notes on the facing pages keyed by line number for easy reference.

Each edition contains an introduction, biographical information, a discussion of the Shakespearean theatre, summaries of each scene, and illustrations from the Folger collection.

Comedies

All's Well That Ends Well	W • 0104
As You Like It*	45703
The Comedy of Errors	W • 0107
Cymbeline	W • 0126
Love's Labor's Lost	W • 0114
Measure for Measure*	45720
The Merchant of Venice*	45721
The Merry Wives of Windsor	W • 0128
A Midsummer Night's Dream*	45723
Much Ado about Nothing*	45724
The Taming of the Shrew*	45730
The Tempest*	45731
Twelfth Night	W • 0124
The Two Gentlemen of Verona	W • 0130
Troilus and Cressida	W • 0103
The Winter's Tale	W • 0102

Poetry

Shakespeare's Sonnets	W • 0132

Tragedies

Antony and Cleopatra	W • 0105
Coriolanus	W • 0125
Hamlet*	45707
Julius Caesar*	45716
King Lear*	45717
Macbeth*	45719
Othello	45225
Pericles	W • 0139
Romeo and Juliet	W • 0121
Titus Andronicus	W • 0141
Timon of Athens	W • 0140

Histories

Henry IV, Part I*	45708
Henry IV, Part II	W • 0110
Henry V*	45710
Henry VI, Part I	W • 0134
Henry VI, Part II	W • 0135
Henry VI, Part III	W • 0136
Henry VIII	W • 0137
King John	W • 0138
Richard II*	45727
Richard III*	45728

Shakespeare for Everyman

By Louis B. Wright. An illuminating introduction to Shakespeare for the general reader. Annotated bibliography, index, extensive illustrations from the Folger collection. W • 1081/90¢

Starred titles 50¢; all others 45¢.

WSP
ⓌWASHINGTON SQUARE PRESS